THE SIMON & SCHUSTER
POCKET GUIDE TO
SHELLS
OF THE WORLD

KENNETH R. WYE

A Fireside Book
Published by Simon & Schuster Inc.
New York London Toronto Sydney Tokyo

Copyright © 1989 Mitchell Beazley Publishers

A Fireside Book
Published by Simon & Schuster Inc.
Simon & Schuster Building
Rockefeller Center
1230 Avenue of the Americas
New York, New York 10020

FIRESIDE and colophon are registered trademarks
of Simon & Schuster Inc.

Edited and designed by Mitchell Beazley International Ltd,
Artists House, 14–15 Manette Street, London W1V 5LB

Simultaneously published in Great Britain by Mitchell Beazley
Publishers

Editor   Richard Dawes
Art Editor   Mike Brown
Production   Stewart Bowling
Executive Editor   Robin Rees

Photographs by Steve Gorton
Artwork by John Hutchinson

Typeset and prepared by Servis Filmsetting Ltd, Manchester
Origination by Scantrans (Singapore)
Printed in Hong Kong

10 9 8 7 6 5 4 3 2 1

Library of Congress Cataloging in Publication Data

Available upon request

ISBN: 0 671 68263 6

C O N T E N T S

AUTHOR'S INTRODUCTION

It is perhaps surprising, with the ever-growing interest in collecting shells and the many books on the subject, that the vast majority of people know little or nothing about them. And yet, when their beautiful colour, form, and incredible variety of species are experienced, who can fail to marvel at these creatures which for centuries have fascinated and been of service to mankind?

Many shells are indeed spectacular in appearance and people sometimes have difficulty in believing that they occur naturally, while other species are, to some eyes, dull or even ugly. But all are natural miracles and each is adapted to its own way of life.

From early times shellfish have provided food for many peoples of the world – and they continue to do so, representing a

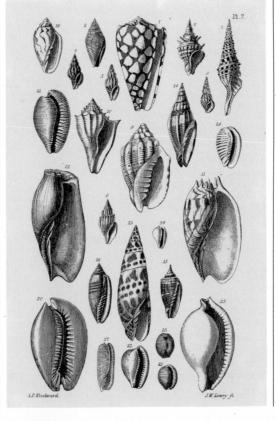

Plates from *A Manual of the Mollusca* 1851–6 by S.P. Woodward

valuable source of income. They have long served as adornment too, and not just in primitive cultures, for the demand for jewellery based on or incorporating shells ensures a profitable shellcraft industry in most developed nations.

But this kind of interest is only a small part of the widespread enthusiasm that shells generate, for all over the world there are collectors and natural historians whose lives are daily involved with them. Whether shells are recovered from coasts on which they have been washed up, empty of their snail-like former occupants, retrieved from shallow high-tide zones, or dredged up from the abyssal depths of the ocean, they provide endless pleasure and knowledge to those who collect and study them.

Starting a collection of shells is easy for, apart from those which can be found on any beach, shells can be bought from specialist shops. Some enthusiasts maintain that every shell collected should be accompanied by details of its scientific name, its geographical range, its habitat, and so on. But each collector should decide how to display and enjoy his or her collection.

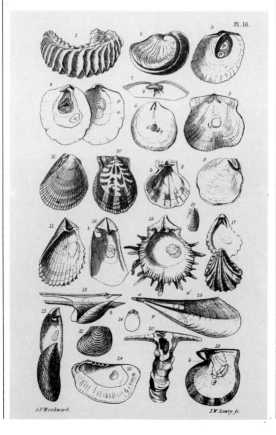

S.P.Woodward.   J.W.Lowry fc.

THE MOLLUSCS

All living creatures are classified into major groups known collectively as phyla. Expert opinion differs as to how many types of mollusc comprise the phylum Mollusca but, taken together, land and marine molluscs probably number more than 100,000 species. Of this total, the marine molluscs, which are the subject of this book, account for about half.

The word "mollusc" derives from the Latin word "mollis", meaning "soft". Molluscs are invertebrate animals – hence the name – with unsegmented bodies generally comprising a head, a foot, a visceral hump or mass containing the internal organs, and a mantle. The shell provides the mollusc with support and protection. This vast group of creatures is better understood when subdivided into six sub-groups, or classes:

Gastropoda

The largest class of mollusc with over 35,000 described species, about half of which are marine. It includes limpets, murex, cowries, cones, volutes, and other families. These soft-bodied snails have tentacles, eyes, a broad, flat foot, and a mantle. The visceral mass is contained in a one-piece, hard shell, which is usually coiled. Most of the Gastropoda, or gastropods, are mobile. The familiar garden snail is a gastropod too.

Bivalvia

The second largest class, in which there are possibly 10,000 species, comprises shells with two pieces, or valves, which are hinged by a supple ligament. Internal muscles control the opening and closing of these valves. Most bivalves have a large foot, a pair of siphons, and a mantle, and most are sessile (they do not move), although a few are highly active. Other creatures in this class include oysters, mussels, clams, and cockles. The Giant Clam, *Tridacna gigas*, grows to over 1 metre/3 feet 3 inches and weighs over 200 kilograms/450 pounds.

Cephalopoda

These highly mobile species are all carnivorous and possess large, complex eyes, a highly developed central nervous system, a powerful, beak-like mouth, and tentacles with suckers. Included in this class are octopods, nautilus, cuttlefish, and squid. They bear little resemblance to other molluscs – certainly as far as their soft parts are concerned. A few possess exterior shells, others, as a result of adaptation and development, have interior shells, while yet others have no shell at all. There are about 400 species, but over 10,000 fossil forms.

Polyplacophora

Chitons, or coat-of-mail shells, are even less like other molluscs than Cephalopoda. Their shell consists of eight, segmented, often ornately patterned, plates, encircled and held together by a leathery girdle. The shells are generally oval and elongate, with either a broad or a narrow foot. Polyplacophorans lack tentacles, but possess micro-sensory organs in the shell and the surface of the girdle. There are about 600 species.

Scaphopoda

"Tusk" or "tooth" shells, the most primitive of all marine molluscs, form a class of 200–400 species. They have a one-piece, tubular, tusk-like shell, open at both ends. The posterior, narrower end generally protrudes above the sand in which they live. No head, eyes, or gills are present, but tusk shells possess a large foot and a tongue.

Monoplacophora

Gastroverms or segmented limpets, as these creatures are known, were at one time believed long extinct, but now almost a dozen species are known, all of which inhabit very deep water. Extremely primitive creatures, they all resemble cap-shaped limpets, with soft, segmented body parts. All species are exceptionally rare.

Gastropod anatomy

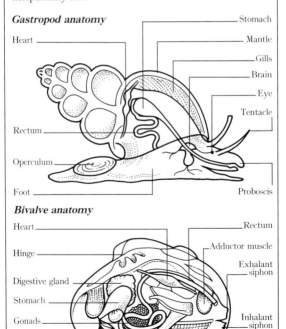

Bivalve anatomy

7

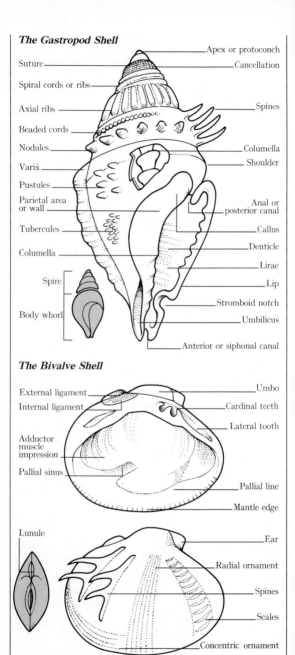

The Gastropod Shell

Apex or protoconch
Suture
Cancellation
Spiral cords or ribs
Axial ribs
Spines
Beaded cords
Nodules
Columella
Varix
Shoulder
Pustules
Parietal area or wall
Anal or posterior canal
Tubercules
Callus
Columella
Denticle
Lirae
Spire
Lip
Stromboid notch
Body whorl
Umbilicus
Anterior or siphonal canal

The Bivalve Shell

External ligament
Umbo
Internal ligament
Cardinal teeth
Lateral tooth
Adductor muscle impression
Pallial sinus
Pallial line
Mantle edge

Lunule
Ear
Radial ornament
Spines
Scales
Concentric ornament

8

THE
HABITAT OF
SHELLS

Seashells live in a wide range of habitats, from the high-water mark on coasts down to extremely deep water. They are adapted to almost any place where the water offers an adequate supply of food. The majority of species worldwide, and certainly the more highly coloured and patterned types, inhabit shallower water.

The sea and the shore can be roughly divided as follows:

SHELL HABITAT ZONES	
Intertidal	The area between the levels of the high and the low tides (also known as the "littoral" zone, from the Latin word for "shore").
Subtidal	The depths below the low-tide mark, including continental shelves and coral reefs down to 100m (330ft) (also known as the shallow-water zone).
Abyssal	The cold, lightless depths which extend to the ocean floor.

Many bivalve groups and species such as mitres and olives thrive in sand or in muddy habitats, while a large number of burrowing shells, including many gastropods, and tusk shells, also find sand ideal. Mangrove swamps are another food-rich habitat attractive to many different species.

On rocky shorelines, where rough water conditions often prevail, species such as limpets, chitons, and top shells are found. These are all adapted to cling to rocks and boulders and all possess strong shells. Other, less robust, species live under rocks or in their crevices.

Many bivalves, among them oysters and clams, produce a byssus, a bundle of hair-like strands, which enable them to cling to the surface on which they live. Coral reefs, usually rich in food, are also a haven for molluscan life and it is there that most of the attractive and highly coloured shells are found. Soft, plant-like corals and sea-fans are home to many molluscan species. Other species live under corals, in coral sand, or in worn coral rubble.

Pelagic species live on or near the surface of the sea, often far from the shore. The Common Purple Snail, *Janthina janthina*, is a typical example, spending its life floating on a raft of bubbles on the open sea.

Abyssal species are usually thinner shells, often white or with minimal colour. Also found in this area, but also in shallower waters, are the Cephalopods such as *Nautilus* and squids. These are highly mobile, swimming around in search of prey.

THE
CLASSIFICATION
OF SHELLS

Although almost all described living creatures have a scientific Latin name, it is, not surprisingly, their common names that are most widely used, and seashells are no exception to this. Most are happy to use names like cockle, whelk, or conch, but the main problem with using common names is that they vary from country to country, not just linguistically but in what they describe. Thus a "conch" in one country could be a "helmet" in another, while cockles and mussels might both be termed "clams" elsewhere. For this reason, a Latin-based nomenclature, or system of naming, has been adopted universally by the scientific fraternity and all those concerned with the accurate description of species. If one species has only one name peculiar to itself, it cannot be mistaken for another or misclassified, and this holds good for anywhere in the world.

Until the middle of the 18th century, when the pioneering work of the Swedish naturalist Carl von Linné, or Linnaeus as he is generally called, became known, there existed a chaos of alternative names for living creatures. In the tenth edition of his momentous *Systema Naturae*, published in 1758, Linnaeus extended the coverage of his earlier works by listing and describing every animal and plant known to him, using two names for each. This system, known as the Binomial System, provided for the first time a consistent nomenclature for the natural world. Common names die hard and it was not until the end of his century that Linnaeus's system was widely accepted.

As an illustration of how this system applies to shells, let us take the example of what is commonly known as the Tiger Cowrie. The scientific name for this shell is *Cypraea tigris*. The first word is the generic name, which links all species belonging to a group known as a genus; the second is the specific name. A generic name cannot be used for more than one group, while the specific name cannot be applied to any other species in that

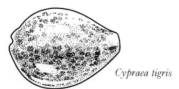

Cypraea tigris

particular genus. Thus *Cypraea tigris* refers to one particular species in one particular genus – and to no other creature.

Just as related species are grouped into genera (the plural of genus) so related genera are placed within a family. The number of genera in a family can range from one to any quantity. The family is in turn placed within a superfamily and the superfamily within an order. The next grouping in order of magnitude is the class, and finally there is the phylum, which we encountered above in introducing seashells as members of the phylum Mollusca. Further subdivisions, such as subgenus and subspecies, are sometimes employed, but these can be confusing to the non-specialist. The following table shows how *Cypraea tigris* is classified within its phylum:

Phylum	Mollusca
Class	Gastropoda
Order	Montocardia
Superfamily	Cypraeacea
Family	Cypraeidae
Genus	*Cypraea*
Species	*tigris*

Latin generic and species names are, when printed, given in italics. The genus name always begins with a capital letter, the species name usually with a lower-case (small) letter. Sometimes varieties, which may just be local variations, are ranked as subspecies. For example, a giant variety of *Cypraea tigris* found only in Hawaiian waters has been named *Cypraea tigris schilderiana*. The name of the subspecies in such cases also begins with a lower-case letter. For every species so classified there is an author – the scientist or other person who first published a valid description of the species and named it, usually in a scientific journal. The date of the publication of the name is usually, but not necessarily, given. So *Cypraea tigris* Linné 1758 was first described and named by Linnaeus in 1758. It must be explained that of all the authors' names, that of Linné/Linnaeus is the only one that may be abbreviated, to "L", which is the form adopted in this book.

"Type" specimens are those original shells on which the author bases his description, while the example he chooses for description is known as the "holotype". All others in the same group in front of him are designated "paratypes". Each holotype must be deposited in a museum in order that it can be referred to in the future for purposes of research and study.

Many of the larger genera, such as *Cypraea* and *Conus*, have at various times and in various books been divided into subgenera – for example, *Erosaria* and *Luria* in the case of *Cypraea*, and *Asprella*, *Lithoconus*, and *Leptoconus* in the case of *Conus*. The current trend, however, is towards simplification and the two genera in this example are usually not subdivided. Taxonomy, the scientific term for classification of the kind described above, has its fashions, like most human activities, and while there are those keen to revise periodically the system of naming shells, there are always those equally determined to resist change. Most often, the battle is between the "splitters" and the "lumpers", the former being keen on listing as many genera and subspecies as possible, the latter maintaining that all "split" forms should simply be subsumed under one major group.

The identification chart on pages 12–13 shows the characteristic shape of a shell within a particular superfamily. It is useful for comparing at a glance the shapes of shells and can also be used to locate an unidentified species. When you have found in the chart the shape of the shell you are trying to identify, turn to the relevant superfamily and scan through the shells until you find the one you are looking for.

IDENTIFICATION CHARTS

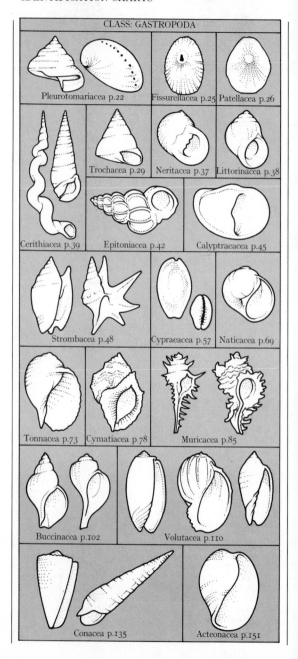

CLASS: GASTROPODA

Pleurotomariacea p.22 · Fissurellacea p.25 · Patellacea p.26

Trochacea p.29 · Neritacea p.37 · Littorinacea p.38

Cerithiacea p.39 · Epitoniacea p.42 · Calyptraeacea p.45

Strombacea p.48 · Cypraeacea p.57 · Naticacea p.69

Tonnacea p.73 · Cymatiacea p.78 · Muricacea p.85

Buccinacea p.102 · Volutacea p.110

Conacea p.135 · Acteonacea p.151

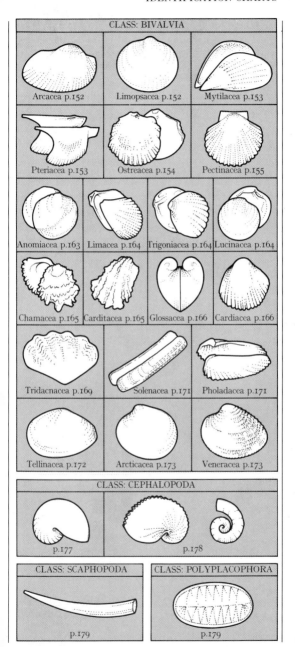

CLASS: BIVALVIA

Arcacea p.152

Limopsacea p.152

Mytilacea p.153

Pteriacea p.153

Ostreacea p.154

Pectinacea p.155

Anomiacea p.163

Limacea p.164

Trigoniacea p.164

Lucinacea p.164

Chamacea p.165

Carditacea p.165

Glossacea p.166

Cardiacea p.166

Tridacnacea p.169

Solenacea p.171

Pholadacea p.171

Tellinacea p.172

Arcticacea p.173

Veneracea p.173

CLASS: CEPHALOPODA

p.177

p.178

CLASS: SCAPHOPODA

p.179

CLASS: POLYPLACOPHORA

p.179

13

DISTRIBUTION

In the mid-19th century S.P. Woodward illustrated the distribution of shells with a map of sixteen zoogeographical provinces, as below. The designations in parentheses are those used in this book for purposes of more precise location.

1 Aleutian (Alaska)
2 Arctic (Arctic Ocean)
3 Australian (Southern, Western, and Eastern Australia, New Zealand)
4 Boreal (Eastern Canada, Northern Atlantic, North Sea)
5 Californian (Western USA)
6 Caribbean (West Indies, Caribbean Sea, Venezuela, Northeastern Brazil, Florida)
7 Indo-Pacific (Philippines, Polynesia, Indonesia, Indian

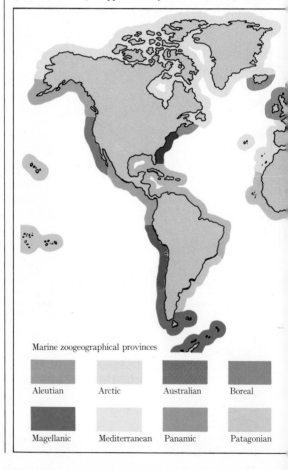

Marine zoogeographical provinces

Aleutian	Arctic	Australian	Boreal
Magellanic	Mediterranean	Panamic	Patagonian

Ocean, Taiwan, Papua New Guinea, New Caledonia, New Hebrides, Thailand, Easter Island, Reunion Islands, Marquesas Islands, Solomon Islands, Andaman Sea, Tahiti, Sulu Sea, Southern India, Western and SW Pacific, China Sea, Northwestern Australia, Mauritius, Sri Lanka, Bay of Bengal, Gulf of Oman, Red Sea, Eastern Africa, Hawaii)

8 Japonic (Japan, Korea)
9 Magellanic (Argentina)
10 Mediterranean (Mediterranean Sea, Northwestern Africa)
11 Panamic (Western Mexico, Western Central America, Western South America)
12 Patagonian (Eastern South America)
13 Peruvian (Western South America)
14 South African (Southern Africa)
15 Transatlantic (Southern and Southwestern USA)
16 West African (Western Africa)

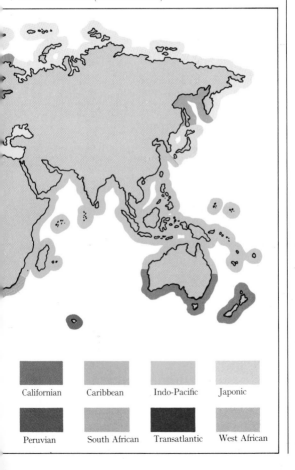

| Californian | Caribbean | Indo-Pacific | Japonic |
| Peruvian | South African | Transatlantic | West African |

CONSERVATION

Many of us are becoming ever more conscious of the need to protect the habitats of living things in order to safeguard their existence – for their own sake, for that of the other organisms with which their lives are inextricably linked, and so that future generations of human beings will be able to enjoy the richness and diversity of the natural world.

Technological and industrial progress exact a high price. In the case of marine life that price is the destruction of habitats by the dumping into the sea on an unprecedented scale of all manner of pollutants and waste products. The algae on which many marine species feed can be destroyed by a variety of effluents, including discarded chemicals, sewage, and, most alarmingly, nuclear waste. Dumping at sea is only one aspect of the problem, however, for our beaches are also being damaged by the negligence and indifference of individuals and large organizations.

Oil pollution is one of the major threats to marine life and leaks from faulty seagoing vessels and large-scale spillages are an established fact. The Persian Gulf, which suffers greatly from this problem, could well be transformed from an area rich in marine creatures to an ecologically dead backwater. Coral reefs, traditionally a treasure trove for shells, suffer not only from pollution but are in some cases blown up by high explosives in order that harbours, airport runways, and other types of construction can be undertaken.

Studies have shown that the survival of molluscs is not greatly affected by collecting for museums or even for the worldwide population of private collectors. On the contrary, it is pollution and direct destruction that pose the real threat to seashells. Even so, the huge scale of shell collecting undertaken in areas like the Philippines and Taiwan in order to meet the demands of the wealthier nations raises the question of whether the seas can survive such wholesale depletion. Many seas still abound in molluscs, yielding up ever greater quantities, but, without controls, can they continue to be so bountiful?

Unfortunately, restricting the flow of shells from certain parts of the world to others would entail its own problems, for in places like the Philippines many local inhabitants are entirely dependent for their livelihood on the produce of the sea. In a situation where Philippine and other shell dealers have yet to recognize the folly of purchasing juvenile shells from fishermen and where the latter are faced with the choice between returning a young shell so that the creature can reproduce and taking the badly needed money for it, there seems to be little real option. Ecological education is the only recourse, for unless the indigent fishermen are made aware of the potentially disastrous effects of overfishing, then they, as well as the shell industry and shell collectors, will suffer.

A related responsibility lies with the collector, who should be constantly aware of the fragile balance of our environment. To this end, certain areas – in Florida and Hawaii, for example – have introduced in recent years restrictions on collecting. The guidelines of the Hawaiian Malacological Society are worth paraphrasing here, for they set a standard to which all collectors would do well to adhere.

Their advice is:

Leave the coral heads alone, for that is not where the shells live. Look instead in the rubble, under the slabs, in the sand, and among loose coral chunks.

Put rock and coral back where and as you found them, even in deep water, for something lives under them and continued exposure will kill it.

Be alert to shell eggs, and protect them, for at best they have a slim chance of survival. Do not take the shell which is guarding them and avoid disturbing breeding groups.

Collect only what you really need and take time to examine your finds. Imperfect or immature shells are of no use to you, so leave them to grow and breed.

Increasing numbers of collectors pursue their hobby gathering only dead specimens, preferring to observe and enjoy living molluscs without disturbing them.

What makes a shell common or rare? Many factors play their part here and during the past two or three centuries the system of grading shells according to their availability on the market has varied considerably. For example, shells which live in very deep water were at one time seldom collected and were therefore considered rare. Modern fishing, dredging, and trawling methods, however, have yielded up more of the contents of deep water and such shells have been regraded as uncommon or even common. Fishing practices can also have the opposite effect in that the mesh size of nets changes or an area containing shells is abandoned for another where the fish yield is better.

Many species are found only in a restricted habitat or in, for example, the waters of remote islands. Such circumstances lead to the shell being difficult to obtain. Politics plays its part too, for countries known to have abundant molluscs but which are politically sensitive, like Cuba, Angola, or North Mozambique, can easily "dry up" as sources, very few shells being collected and even fewer being exported. In the case of the Persian Gulf, a combination of political tension and the harm caused to molluscs by oil and other pollutants will probably render species from that area rare which were formerly considered common or even abundant.

Another factor is the existence of nature reserves and conservation areas, which usually enforce severe restrictions on collecting, if allowing it at all. In such regions as the Red Sea, Australia's Great Barrier Reef, and the Galapagos Islands, species which are locally endemic thus become difficult, if not impossible, to obtain.

The law of supply and demand also has a powerful influence. For example *Cypraea aurantium*, the Golden Cowrie, is reasonably plentiful in localities such as Samar Island, in the Philippines, but, because of its attractiveness and consequent fame, the demand for it outstrips supply.

Yet another factor affecting the status of species is the fact that some shells are regarded as seasonal – occurring only at certain tides, or at certain times of the year. The status of *Argonauta*, for example, has fluctuated widely over long periods – in the past few years very few have been collected in Australian waters where it was previously common, as may well be the case again in the future.

COLLECTING SHELLS

Those who collect shells are not an easily identifiable group, for the degree of commitment to building a collection varies widely. There are casual collectors who pick up "beached" shells when on holiday or visiting coastal regions, there are those who travel to established collecting areas in their own country or overseas, those who own boats and visit less well-known spots to fish for shells, those prepared to skindive or scuba dive for them, and those no less committed collectors who buy all their specimens through reputable dealers. Similarly, collectors embrace both those who are genuinely happy with a dull or chipped shell, as long as it is of the species they are looking for, and those who will accept nothing but the best specimens for their cabinets and who spend hours looking at them through a high-powered magnifying glass or measuring them with Vernier callipers.

Nowadays it is the fashion among serious collectors to specialize in one group or particular type of shell. This is probably due to the overwhelming range of shells currently available, which can make collecting more problematic than enjoyable. But it may also have something to do with the space needed for a comprehensive collection. With living space at a premium in most developed countries, it can be difficult simply to find or afford room for a large collection. Consequently, many collectors content themselves with small, intimate groups of shells such as the olives or the marginellas. Another type of collector takes an interest only in so-called "micro-shells". These are shells of no more than around 1cm ($\frac{1}{2}$in) in the mature state. Since many species are only 1 or 2mm long, sorting and classifying them can be an exacting and time-consuming task.

Another approach is to seek out abnormal specimens. Although the natural world is a marvel of organization, it would be incomplete without freakish forms, whether these be true deviations from the norm or just the result of accidents or predation. Thus some shells are heavily scarred, others develop long, curved, or otherwise bizarre spires, and yet others have strange sculpturing, all of which can enhance a shell in the eyes of some collectors. Abnormal coloration, such as the black in cowries from New Caledonia, possibly caused by cobalt in the water, is no less attractive to some.

Of course, there are still the old favourites, of which cowries are by far the most popular. Next in popularity are cones, volutes, and murex. Cowries in particular require little display space and most are readily obtainable, although the rare species can cost several hundred pounds or dollars and the rarest of all – *Cypraea fultoni*, Fulton's Cowrie – appears on dealers' lists infrequently and when it does a prime specimen can command as much as £5,000 (around US$9,000).

Buying shells

Many collectors buy their first shells from tourist shops at seaside resorts or from shops which do a casual trade in them. However, if the interest takes root they invariably progress to buying from specialist dealers, from whom they can obtain not only a wide choice of species but also valuable advice on collecting, as well as books on the subject and all the paraphernalia of the collector. Some dealers share their interest to the extent of showing customers their own private collections, often containing rare items which are strictly not for sale.

Buying by mail order should be approached with caution, however, since although many such companies are perfectly honest, there are those which sell poor or incorrectly described shells, in some cases having taken the customer's money in advance with a promise of a refund if he or she is not satisfied. It may well prove difficult to hold the unscrupulous dealer to this in the event of dissatisfaction. It pays to ask around about the reputation of a mail-order dealer before buying from him, as indeed it does about the ordinary shop if it is unknown to you.

The cost of shells depends on various factors, the most significant of which is the availability of the species. But it must be borne in mind too that each shell is an individual item and that two shells of the same species can vary greatly in quality and therefore in price. Do not forget either that the dealer's overhead costs, based largely on the location and size of his shop, will also affect the price of shells.

Abundant and common species can cost from under 50 pence($1) to £5 (US$9), while uncommon varieties may cost up to £50 (US$90). Many rare species sell for between £100 and £500 (US$175–900) and, in a few cases, the price is well in excess of £1,000 (US$1,750) and may be several times greater.

To enable collectors to buy shells with some degree of confidence, many dealers have adopted an international system of grading shells for sale. The criteria are as follows.

Gem – A perfect specimen, adult and without visible breaks or flaws. The spire must be perfect, the lips unchipped and not filed, and the spines unbroken. There must be no excessive oiling and the specimen should be well cleaned.

Fine – An adult shell with only minor flaws or with no more than one shallow growth scar. It must bear the original colour and gloss. The outer lip or edge may have one small crack or chip and, in the case of *Murex* or *Spondylus*, a spine may be slightly broken. There should be no repairs and the shell should be well cleaned.

Fair or good – A reasonable shell with few flaws. It will have growth scars, broken spines, or a worn lip or spire. The shell can be sub-adult but should display the typical characteristics of the species.

Poor – A shell of so-called "commercial" grade. It will be worn, faded, broken, chipped, or holed, and whatever flaws it has will be obvious.

Some shells come with just an indication of the country, or possibly the more precise region, of origin. Others are accompanied by full data: detailed notes on the place of origin, the depth at which the species lives, the type of habitat, the date of collection, and the original collector's name. Where data is not available and the customer requires it, some dealers will assist in compiling it. Other purchasers are not at all concerned by the lack of data, as long as they know roughly what part of the world the shell came from.

There are those who buy shells in the belief that they are an investment, but, usually, those shells which were comparatively rare have become more common and so less valuable. Although a few shells, such as *Cypraea aurantium*, Golden Cowrie, and *Cypraea broderipii*, Broderip's Cowrie, have held their price, many others have lost value. At the time of writing the only species which seems to be rising in both demand and value is *Cypraea fultoni*. Fulton's Cowrie. It is a fact too that in time shells lose their pristine condition, often becoming rather dull in appearance. The best advice, unless you are a gambler by nature, is to collect simply for pleasure – nothing more, nothing less.

A good collection of shells usually entails the expenditure of much time and possibly a considerable amount of money. Therefore it is only sensible to provide appropriate storage and display facilities for it. The casual shell "fancier" may keep the shells on open shelves or on the coffee table, but the serious collector takes care to protect them from sunlight, which can cause shells to fade, by using purpose-made drawers or cases. Many collectors achieve the same protection by adapting chests of drawers or other items of furniture or by keeping the shells in simple containers in shady places, even lofts or garages!

The uses of shells
The significance of shells to mankind is of course not restricted to their collection. Long before shells were coveted for their beauty, their occupants provided food. The shells of cockles, oysters, limpets, and other edible species have been found in piles of waste discarded thousands of years ago. Among the first to cultivate shelled creatures for food were the Romans, who farmed oysters and land snails.

The indigenous population of the Indo-Pacific region and the Americas have eaten molluscan species since early times, and while present-day Californians favour abalones, on the east coast clam chowder and Cherrystone Clams are very popular. All over the world shells form the basis of many dishes, from the humble but nourishing whelk to the Japanese delicacy of *Cypraea tigris* roasted alive on coals or the Coquilles St Jacques enjoyed in smart restaurants everywhere.

Shells have also been used as currency, notably in Asia, Central Africa, the islands of the Indian Ocean, and Malaysia. The favoured species were *Cypraea moneta* and *Cypraea annulus*, both cowries, for their size makes them easy to handle and to string together. They are still used for trading in primitive societies. North American Indians ground down pieces of bivalve shells (usually *Mercenaria*) and used them as "wampum", for bartering, while tusk shells were used for trading in the USA and Canada until the mid-19th century. In various parts of the world, long-distance trade routes have been identified because of the presence of shells from far-off places.

Throughout history seashells have served a wide variety of other purposes, one of the best-documented of which is the production of dyes, but the principal commercial use nowadays is in shellcraft. In areas such as Taiwan and the Philippines there are well established industries producing shell-based jewellery and other items, some practical, others simply decorative. Mother of Pearl remains highly popular for earrings, brooches, hairslides, and suchlike, but there is an ever-increasing variety of artifacts available and manufacturers are constantly looking out for previously unexploited species which they can fashion into saleable objects.

THE SHELLS
IN COLOUR

The arrangement of the shells on pages 22–179 follows the conventional system of classification. The species, which, as we have seen, all belong to the phylum Mollusca, are divided by class, superfamily, and family. The heading in bold type at the top of each page gives the superfamily (or superfamilies) described on that page. The heading in light type above the superfamily heading gives the class in which the shells on that page are found. Within each page the shells are divided into families and a heading in bold type indicates the beginning of the coverage of a family. If you wish to use the book to identify a shell, then turn to the identification charts on pages 12–13 and match up as near as possible the profile of your specimen with that of a superfamily, and then scan the pages referred to to locate your shell.

The name that you will see at the head of the caption for each species gives its generic name and its specific name. As long as you know its generic name or the specific name, you can find a shell by locating either of these names in the index. If you know only the common name, you will also find this indexed. Bear in mind, however, that not all the species described in this book have a common name, although every shell has a universally adopted scientific name.

The author of the species – the person who first published a valid description of the species and named it – and the date of publication are the next piece of information.

The size of each shell listed in this book is given in both metric and Imperial measurements and represents the average size of mature specimens of the species. In the case of shells with long, projecting spines, such as *Murex* and *Spondylus*, the size includes the spines. Likewise, in the case of *Xenophoras*, the shells' attachments are included in the figures given. The correspondence between metric and Imperial measurements is approximate, to avoid the use of small fractions in Imperial measurements.

The geographical range of the species is given next. You will find the distribution map on pages 14–15 useful.

The availability of each species is given in an abbreviated form which is explained by the key below.

KEY TO AVAILABILITY

A. Abundant – A well-established species found in large numbers and usually in very accessible habitats. Most likely to be available commercially.

C. Common – A species found readily in both accessible collecting areas and in commercial outlets.

U. Uncommon – A species which is not always readily available commercially. Its habitats may be localized, restricted, or not readily accessible because of, for example, deep or difficult water, or substrates.

R. Rare – A species seldom available commercially, and thus potentially costly, because found only in deep or dangerous water or on a very difficult subterrain, or in extremely localized or inaccessible habitats.

Pleurotomariidae Commonly called slit shells from the characteristic anal slit which permits the passage of water and waste matter, these shells were known as fossils until the mid-nineteenth century, when they were first fished from the Caribbean. About sixteen species of this biologically primitive snail are recognized today. Possibly the oldest group of molluscs, dating back to the early Cambrian period, they variously inhabit the very deep waters of the Caribbean, the area off eastern South Africa, the Atlantic off eastern South America, and oriental regions of the Indo-Pacific seas, in many cases to depths of 100–600m (330–1970ft). All species are vegetarian.

Pleurotomariidae are quite large and of a rounded, conical, coiled shape, with numerous whorls. All have a horny operculum.

1 *PLEUROTOMARIA AFRICANA* **African Slit Shell** *Tomlin 1948* to (12cm/4¾in) *South Africa* ***R***. A much thinner, lighter, and more delicate shell than *Pleurotomaria hirasei*. It is pale beige or orange and is fished from depths of 200–400m (655–1310ft).
2 *PLEUROTOMARIA HIRASEI* **The Emperor's Slit Shell** *Pilsbury 1903* (10cm/4in) *Japan and Taiwan* ***R***. The most common species of the group, a rather thick and heavy shell. It is deep red and orange, with fine spiral cords and beading, and the operculum is round.

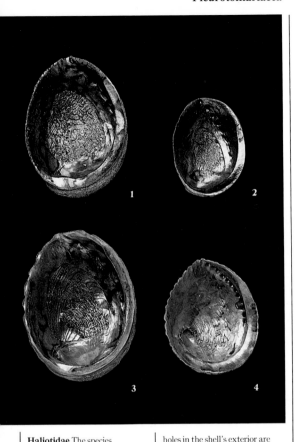

Haliotidae The species comprising this family (there are around a hundred) are also known as abalones, sea ears, or ormers. They are flat and round or oval, with a flat spire, and their size range is 2–30cm/⅞–12in. All the species have mother-of-pearl interiors and water and waste matter are expelled through a series of holes on the body whorl. Their habitat ranges from low-tide zones to depths of several hundred metres and they are usually found in shallow water, firmly attached to rocks.

1 *HALIOTIS FULGENS* **Green Abalone** *Philippi 1845* (to 20cm/8in) *S California to Mexico* **C**. The interior is of a beautiful, iridescent green and there is a large, prominent muscle scar. Sponge holes in the shell's exterior are common.

2 *HALIOTIS IRIS* **Paua Abalone** *Martyn 1784* (12cm/4¾in) *New Zealand* **C**. Paua is the Maori name for abalone. The shell has a deep blue-green interior and the nacre is used for jewellery.

3 *HALIOTIS RUFESCENS* **Red Abalone** *Swainson 1822* (to 30cm/12in) *S California to Mexico* **C**. The exterior is red and extends in a thin band over the margins to a nacreous interior. There is a conspicuous muscle scar.

4 *HALIOTIS MIDAE* **Midas Ear Abalone** *L. 1758* (to 17cm/6¾in) *South Africa* **C**. Commercially fished in great numbers, this shell has a silver mother-of-pearl interior and a deeply ridged exterior, often encrusted.

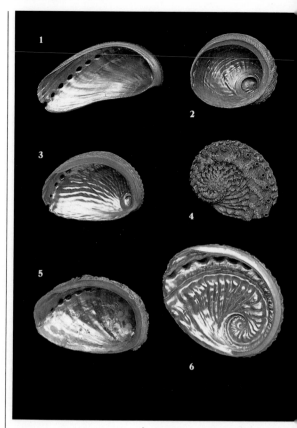

1 *HALIOTIS ASININA* **Ass's Ear** *L. 1758* (10cm/4in) *Central Indo-Pacific* **A**. An elongated, curved, and smooth shell, with little or no sculpturing. The interior is silver nacre and the exterior, which is polished for commercial purposes, green-brown.

2 *HALIOTIS CYCLOBATES* **Whirling Abalone** *Péron 1816* (6cm/2¼in) *S Australia* **C**. The initial whorl is set deep within the pearly interior of this species which lives on rocks and occasionally on other mollusc shells.

3 *HALIOTIS AUSTRALIS* **Austral** *Gmelin 1791* (8cm/3¼in) *New Zealand* **C**. Ranging from pale beige to green, this shell has low, evenly spaced spiral ridges. It is known locally as the Silver Paua.

4 and 6 *HALIOTIS SCALARIS* **Staircase Abalone** *Leach 1814* (10cm/4in) *S and W Australia* **U**. A very delicately sculptured and beautiful species with deep red-orange spiral ridges and fissures on the exterior. Large specimens in collectable condition are hard to find. The interior and exterior are shown here.

5 *HALIOTIS TUBERCULATA* **European Edible Abalone** *L. 1758* (9cm/3½in) *Mediterranean and NE Atlantic* **A**. The interior is silver pearl and the exterior is often encrusted with lime deposits or small barnacles. A popular food source in the Channel Islands, the species is known there as the ormer.

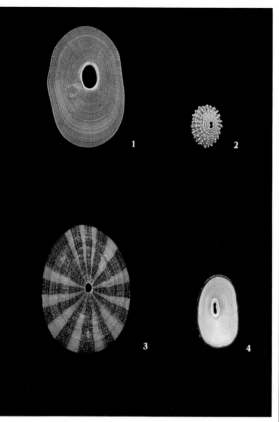

Fissurellidae The so-called keyhole limpets have flat, oval or round shells like those of true limpets, with a natural hole at the top or, in some cases, a slit on the margin. A mantle covers the shell of the living creature, but no species possesses an operculum. The members of this family inhabit rocky areas and coral below the low-tide mark in the warmer seas of the world and all are vegetarian.

1 *MEGATHURA CRENULATA* **Great Keyhole Limpet** *Sowerby 1825* (12cm/4¾in) *California to Mexico* **C**. A sizeable species with a large oval hole surrounded by grey-beige radially ridged shell. The margins are minutely crenulated and the interior is pure white.

2 *FISSURELLA NODOSA* **Knobbed Keyhole Limpet** *Born 1778* (3cm/1¼in) *Florida and West Indies* **C**. The exterior has coarse, nodulose ridges with a figure-of-eight hole. The interior is pure white.

3 *FISSURELLA MAXIMA* **Giant Keyhole Limpet** *Sowerby 1835* (12cm/4¾in) *W South America* **C**. Red-brown rays on a cream background radiate from a central hole. The interior is white.

4 *FISSURELLA CRASSA* **Thick Keyhole Limpet** *Lamarck 1822* (8cm/3¼in) *W Central to South America* **C**. A thick-shelled species with a long, narrow slit which is in some cases edged with pink. A brown rim is visible when the shell is seen from beneath.

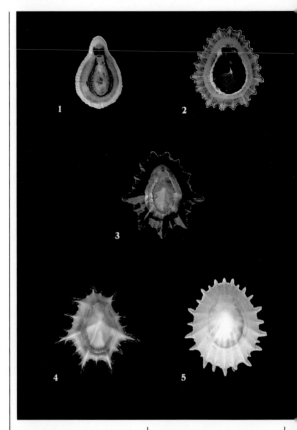

Patellidae Limpets are a large group of flat or conical shells with no hole at the apex. All are shore rock dwellers (and difficult to remove once disturbed) and are vegetarian.

1 *PATELLA COCHLEAR* **Spoon Limpet** *Born 1778* (6cm/2¼in) *South Africa* **C**. A spoon- or pear-shaped species with a striking grey-blue scar area with a white margin. The exterior is often encrusted with lime.

2 *PATELLA GRANATINA* **Sandpaper Limpet** *L. 1758* (8cm/3¼in) *South Africa* **C**. The interior is rich brown and there is a central scar with a pale ring that blends into cream, orange, and even bluish tints to the margin.

3 *PATELLA OCULUS* **Eye Limpet** *Born 1778* (10cm/4in) *W South*

Africa **C**. A striking shell with a pink-brown central scar ringed with white and a dark-brown surround to the margins. The ribbed exterior has peripheral star-like points.

4 *PATELLA LONGICOSTA* **Star Limpet** *Lamarck 1819* (8cm/3¼in) *South Africa* **C**. An aptly named species popular with collectors. Strong exterior ribs extend from the apex to the pointed margin. A large cream-orange central scar blends into white with blue undertones to the margin.

5 *PATELLA BARBARA L. 1758* (10cm/4in) *South Africa* **C**. A variable species, some examples having strong ribs, others finer or more numerous ribs. The exterior is creamy white, the interior white with a pale cream scar.

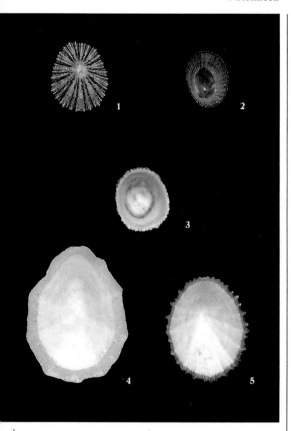

1 *PATELLA MINIATA* **Cinnabar Limpet** *Born 1778* (to 3cm/1¼in) *South Africa* **C**. A thin and delicately patterned and sculptured variety, often having vivid red-brown or pink striped radiating patterns or lines on the exterior. It inhabits the intertidal zone.

2 *NACELLA DEAURATA* **Copper Limpet** *Gmelin 1791* (5cm/2in) *SE South America* **C**. An oval, high-domed shell which is slightly compressed at the rear end. The interior is golden nacreous and the exterior is ridged. It is found in the intertidal zone and occasionally on seaweed.

3 *PATELLA VULGATA* **Common European Limpet** *L. 1758* (6cm/2¼in) *N Atlantic* **A**. An edible species found throughout the British Isles on rocky coasts. The shell sculpturing and pattern vary and the interior is creamy white.

4 *PATELLA MEXICANA* **Giant Mexican Limpet** *Broderip and Sowerby 1829* (to 30cm/12in) *W Central America* **C**. The largest known species in the limpet family, it is found on rocks in shallow water. The interior is creamy white and porcelain-like, with a darker margin, and the exterior is often encrusted.

5 *PATELLA TABULARIS* **Tabular Limpet** *Krauss 1848* (13cm/5¼in) *South Africa* **C**. The largest of the African limpets, it is found on rocks, the biggest specimens being exposed during equinoctial spring tides.

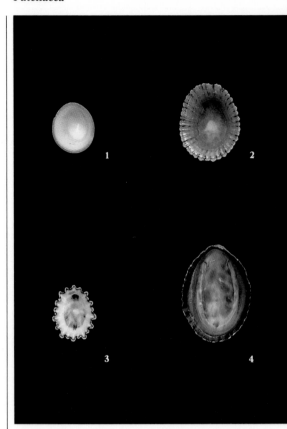

Acmaeidae There are slight biological differences between this family and the Patellidae, but the shells are generally similar, being round, oval, or irregular. They normally do not have the mother-of-pearl or nacreous interior characteristic of the Patellidae, but one that is porcellaneous.
1 *ACMAEA MITRA* **White Cap Limpet** *Rathke 1833* (2.5cm/1in) *Alaska to Mexico* **C**. A subtidal rock dweller with a porcellaneous, smooth white interior, a dirty beige exterior, and a domed apex.
2 *PATELLOIDA TRAMOSERICA* **Ariel Limpet** *Holten 1802* (5cm/2in) *S Australia* **C**. Found on intertidal rocky shores, this shell has a finely ridged dorsum and is often encrusted. The central scar is greyish with golden and nacreous rays to the margin. There are intermittent black "dashes".
3 *PATELLOIDA ALTICOSTATA* **High-ribbed Limpet** *Angas 1865* (2.5cm/1in) *S Australia* **C**. An intertidal species with an attractive central scar with beige, yellow, and blue tinges. The background is white with a beige or dark-grey crenulated margin and the exterior is ridged.
4 *LOTTIA GIGANTEA* **Giant Owl Limpet** *Sowerby 1834* (8cm/3¼in) *California to Mexico* **C**. The interior is deep brown with near-black margins and there are white splashes around the central scar. This flattish shell is found on shore rocks near the high-tide line.

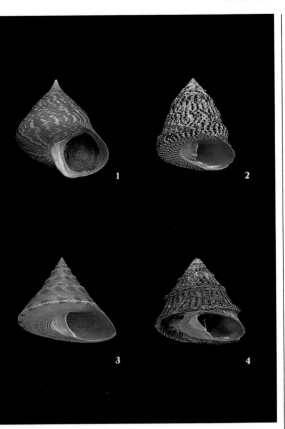

Trochidae This is a large group consisting of hundreds of species with numerous genera and worldwide distribution. The habitat extends from tidal rock pools to abyssal regions. Most species are herbivorous, some feeding on sponges. All are conical and top-shaped, with a nacreous interior. The higher-spired species generally dwell in calmer, sheltered water, the low-spired and flat species in rougher seas.

1 *MAUREA TIGRIS* **Tiger Shell** *Martyn 1784* (6cm/2¼in) *New Zealand U.* A prized collectors' shell found among rocks in subtidal zones. The spire is high, with a large aperture.

2 *TROCHUS VIRGATUS* **Striped Top** *Gmelin 1791* (6cm/2¼in) *Indo-Pacific C.* A thick, solid species with spiral beading of green and red on a white background. It is found on coral reefs and is often lime-encrusted, but careful cleaning is well worthwhile.

3 *CALLIOSTOMA FORMOSENSE* **Formosa Top** *E. A. Smith 1907* (6cm/2¼in) *Taiwan C.* A thin, delicate shell with fine spiral cords and beading. The exterior is reddish-brown and the interior is lavender-coloured and pearly. Found in deep water, it is popular in shell craft.

4 *TEGULA REGINA* **Regal Top** *Stearns 1892* (5cm/2in) *California U.* A thick, grey-black shell with four or five overlapping whorls with axial ribbing. A vivid orange ring exists around the umbilical area and the aperture is yellow.

1 *MONODONTA LABIO* **Toothed
Monodont** *L. 1758* (2.5cm/1in)
Indo-Pacific **A**. A thick and heavy
shell which has a green-brown
tinted background with spiral
beading and zigzags of dark
brown-grey. There is a noticeable
white porcellaneous callus around
an otherwise nacreous aperture.
2 *LISCHKEIA UNDOSA* Kuroda and
Kawamura *1956* (3cm/1¼in)
Philippines **U**. A lightweight, pale
grey-white shell which inhabits
deep waters. It has granulose
spiral cords with larger nodules on
the upper rims of the whorls.
3 *TROCHUS CONUS* **Cone Top**
Gmelin *1791* (7cm/2¾in) *Indo-
Pacific* **C**. A rounded, thick shell
with some spiral beading and
vivid red stripes on a white
background.

4 *BATHYBEMBIX
ARGENTEONITENS* **Silvery
Margarite** *Lischke 1872*
(4cm/1½in) *Japan* **C**. This species
inhabits deep water at 50–400m
(330–1310ft) and is lightweight
with a moderately high spire.
There are nodulose whorls and
the pearly interior shows through.
5 *TECTUS TRISERIALIS* **Tall Top**
Lamarck *1822* (6cm/2⅜in)
Philippines **U**. An elegant tall and
narrow shell encircled with
regular granulose cords and with
a flat, white base.
6 *CALLIOSTOMA CUNNINGHAMI*
Cunningham's Top *Griffith and
Pidgeon 1833* (5cm/2in) *New
Zealand* **C**. Lightweight and thin,
this species has slightly convex
whorls and delicate spiral beads of
red-brown on a beige background.

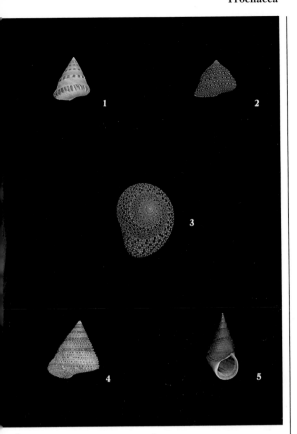

1 *CALLIOSTOMA MONILE* **Monile Top** *Reeve 1863* (to 2cm/⅘in) *W Australia U.* A sturdy but smallish shallow-water dweller with a straight-sided tall spire. Its overall colour is beige, with dominant pink-mauve spots on white bands and very fine spiral striae.
2 *CLANCULUS PUNICEUS* **Strawberry Top** *Philippi 1846* (2cm/⅘in) *E Africa C.* A very popular species of a distinctive bright red with black spots on spiral ridges, this shell is found under rocks in the intertidal zone.
3 *CLANCULUS UNDATUS Lamarck 1816* (to 3cm/1¼in) *S Australia C.* A rounded, flattened shell with a pearly interior. The base colour is brick-red-brown with dark, wavy axial stripes.

4 *CALLIOSTOMA ANNULATUM* **Ringed Top** *Lightfoot 1786* (2cm/⅘in) *California U.* A pretty species popular with collectors. The background is golden-yellow and pearly, with red-pink spiral beading on lavender bands.
5 *PHASIANOTROCHUS EXIMIUS* **Green Jewel Top** *Perry 1811* (3cm/1¼in) *S Australia C.* The interior is vivid green-blue and there is a tall, brown, shiny spire with fine spiral striae. An inhabitant of weeded areas in shallow water.

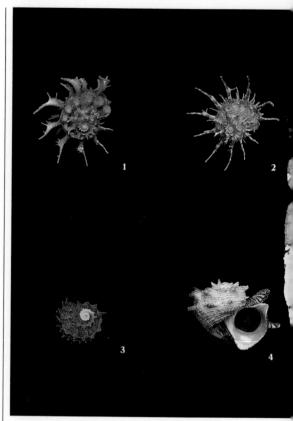

Angaridae The Angarias are popular collectors' items. They all have a depressed spire, an enlarged body whorl, and a horny operculum. These shells are frequently collected heavily encrusted with lime and marine growth. All are vegetarian and some inhabit deep waters.

1 *ANGARIA SPHAERULA* **Kiener's Delphinula** *Kiener 1839* (5cm/2in) *Philippines* **U.** The coloration can be pink, yellow, or bronze, with a nacreous base showing through. The spine growth varies in this attractive species which is trapped in nets in deep, calm waters.

2 *ANGARIA VICDANI* **Victor Dan's Angaria** *Kosuge 1980* (5cm/2in) *Philippines* **U.** A favourite with collectors, but perfect specimens are rare since the long spines are extremely fragile. It is fished from deep waters in tangle nets.

3 *ANGARIA DELPHINUS* **Common Delphinula** *L. 1758* (7cm/2¾in) *Indo-Pacific* **C.** An extremely variable species, both in coloration and sculpturing, it is generally brown-black or dark red beneath an encrustation of lime.

4 *ANGARIA TYRIA* **Tyria Delphinula** *Reeve 1842* (7cm/2¾in) *Australia* **C.** A variable species with a flattened spire and large body whorl and aperture. There are coarse spiral spines and serrations and the coloration is creamy white with a dark brown-black umbilicus.

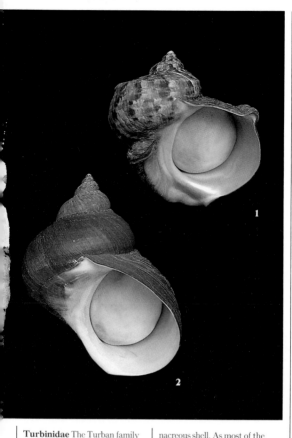

Turbinidae The Turban family comprises several hundred species, most of which are vegetarian and inhabit shallow waters in warm tropical seas. The Turbans are top-shaped and coiled, with large body whorls and apertures. All have thickened calcareous opercula, and many are ornately sculptured or brightly coloured.

1 *TURBO MARMORATUS* **Giant Green Turban** L. *1758* (to 20cm/8in) *Indo-Pacific* **C**. A thick, heavy shell with a large white operculum, the largest of the genus and always thickly encrusted. It has been widely used in the mother-of-pearl industry, originally for buttons, but now beads and jewellery are fashioned from the beautiful thick nacreous shell. As most of the shells are gathered for such uses, collectable specimens are becoming harder to obtain.

2 *TURBO JOURDANI* **Jourdan's Turban** *Kiener 1839* (to 20cm/8in) *S Australia* **U**. The second largest member of the group, this shell inhabits rocks in shallow water. It is lighter than *Turbo marmoratus* and is of a uniformly brown colour, again with a thick white calcareous operculum and mother-of-pearl interior. It is keenly sought after by collectors but its lip edges are often rough or filed.

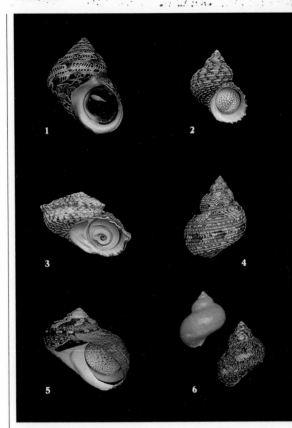

1 *TURBO PETHOLATUS* **Tapestry Turban** *L. 1758* (6cm/2¼in) *Indo-Pacific C.* An ever-popular shell with its thick green operculum known as a "cat's eye".

2 *TURBO PULCHER* **Beautiful Turban** *Reeve 1842* (6cm/2¼in) *W Australia C.* This shallow reef dweller has coarse spiral ribbing with a cream base colour and axial zigzag markings ranging from green to brown. It has a pustulose operculum.

3 *NINELLA WHITLEYI* **Whitley's Turban** *Iredale 1949* (6cm/2¼in) *Australia C.* The base colour is beige-grey with strong spiral cords and fine axial growth ridges. There are nodules on some whorls and a thick operculum with spiral ridges.

4 *TURBO CANALICULATUS* **Channelled Turban** *Hermann 1781* (6cm/2¼in) *Caribbean U.* An attractive Turban with rounded whorls that are sculptured on the upper side with deeply incised spiral grooves.

5 *TURBO SARMATICUS* **South African Turban** *L. 1758* (7cm/2¾in) *South Africa C.* This species is found, often heavily encrusted, on rocky shores. It has a brown periostracum and a white operculum of coarse, tightly packed pustules. A popular commercial shell.

6 *TURBO REEVEI* **Reeve's Turban** *Philippi 1847* (4cm/1½in) *Philippines C.* A shallow reef dweller that is often confused with *Turbo petholatus*, but is usually smaller. Its coloration and pattern vary.

1

2

3

Phasianellidae Pheasant shells form a relatively small family of mostly vegetarian species. They have smooth, colourful exteriors and white, non-nacreous interiors, calcareous operculae, and extremely fragile lips.

1 *PHASIANELLA AUSTRALIS* **Australian Pheasant** *Gmelin 1791* (6cm/2½in) *S Australia* **C**. Popular with collectors, this shell is long and conical and the colour of its pattern extremely variable. The aperture is almond shaped and the operculum white and thickish.

Astraeinae The star shells are a popular family among collectors. They are mostly conical or top shaped, with a flattened base, and have much sculpturing and long spines. All species possess opercula. Star shells are often found heavily encrusted with chalky lime deposits.

2 *ASTRAEA UNDOSA* **Wavy Turban** *Wood 1828* (10cm/4in) *California to Mexico* **C**. This species is possibly the largest of the genus and inhabits tidal rocks. The shell is thick and heavy and the operculum is calcareous, with strong concentric grooves.

3 *ASTRAEA HELIOTROPIUM* **Sunburst Star Shell** *Martyn 1784* (10cm/4in) *New Zealand* **R**. A much sought after deepwater shell reputedly discovered during Captain Cook's voyages to New Zealand. Large, well-cleaned specimens are scarce.

35

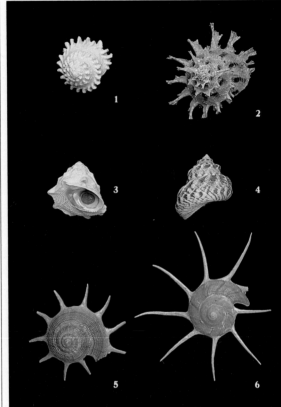

1 *ASTRAEA ROTULARIA* **Rotary Star Shell** *Lamarck 1822* (4cm/1½in) *W Australia C.* A depressed chalky white species with a green-brown operculum which inhabits subtidal rocks. Good, clean specimens are scarce.

2 *BOLMA GIRGYLLUS* **Girgyllus Star Shell** *Reeve 1861* (5cm/2in) *Philippines U.* This favourite with collectors has recently become obtainable from deepwater tangle nets off the central Philippines. Coloration and spine length vary and the operculum is white.

3 *ASTRAEA STELLARE* **Blue-mouthed Star Shell** *Gmelin 1791* (4cm/1½in) *Australia C.* A chalky white, rounded, conical shell with wavy indentations around the edge of the body

whorl. The operculum has possibly the only true blue coloration in the world of shells.

4 *ASTRAEA TUBER* **Green Star Shell** *L. 1767* (5cm/2in) *Caribbean C.* A chunky, thick shell which is generally green-beige. It inhabits subtidal rocks and is often heavily encrusted.

5 *GUILDFORDIA TRIUMPHANS* **Triumphant Star Shell** *Philippi 1841* (6cm/2½in) *Taiwan and Japan C.* A popular deepwater shell of a nacreous beige-bronze and with projecting spines and a white operculum.

6 *GUILDFORDIA YOKA* **Yoka Star Shell** *Jousseaume 1888* (10cm/4in) *Japan to Philippines C.* This collectors' favourite has eight or nine very long spines of striking appearance.

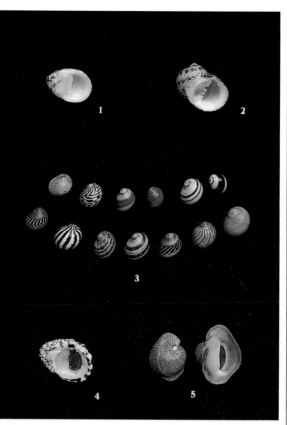

Neritidae The members of this family can store water within their shell and so are able to withstand periods without moisture. Most neritidae are spherical, with large body whorls. The opercula are calcareous and the sculpturing and pattern variable.

1 *NERITA POLITA* **Polished Nerite** *L. 1758* (2.5cm/1in) *Indo-Pacific* **A**. A species with variable pattern and coloration which inhabits rocks in the intertidal zone. The spire is flattened, the surface is smooth and shiny, and the parietal shield is wide and porcellaneous.

2 *NERITA PELORONTA* **Bleeding Tooth Shell** *L. 1758* (3cm/1¼in) *Caribbean* **A**. An inhabitant of shore rocks, this species has an obvious red-orange staining around the parietal teeth and a dark red-brown operculum.

3 *NERITINA COMMUNIS* **Candy Nerite** *Quoy and Gaimard 1832* (1.5cm/⅝in) *Philippines* **A**. A species with an infinite variety of colours and patterns, this shell is found in mangroves.

4 *NERITA TEXTILIS* **Rough Nerite** *Gmelin 1791* (3cm/1¼in) *Indo-Pacific* **C**. Found on shore rocks, this shell has broad black-and-white spiral bands in a zig-zag pattern.

5 *CLYPEOLUM LATISSIMUM* **Wide Nerite** *Broderip 1833* (3cm/1¼in) *W Central America* **C**. This shell inhabits estuaries and the mouths of rivers. It has a wide, flaring mouth and there are fine netted patterns on the dorsum.

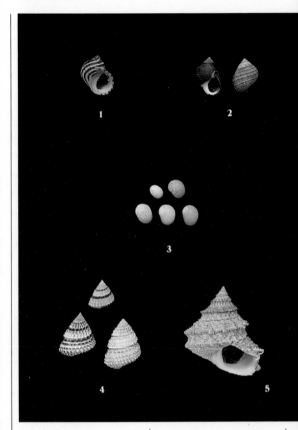

1

2

3

4

5

Littorinidae The periwinkles form a group of over 100 species of smallish shells with a rather drab coloration. All can retain water and endure periods of desiccation by virtue of the tight fit of the operculum. They inhabit rocky shores in most parts of the world, feeding on weeds and algae.

1 *LITTORINA ZEBRA* **Striped Periwinkle** *Donovan 1825* (3cm/1¼in) *Central America* **C**. One of the more colourful members of a generally drab group, this shell inhabits intertidal rocks.

2 *LITTORINA LITTOREA* **Common Periwinkle** *L. 1758* (2cm/⅜in) *N Atlantic* **A**. The well-known edible winkle is widespread on both sides of the Atlantic, and is especially popular as a food in the UK.

3 *LITTORINA LITTORALIS* **Dwarf Periwinkle** *L. 1758* (1cm/⅜in) *N Atlantic* **A**. Found on eastern American as well as European shores, this yellow-orange or beige shell lives in large numbers on rocky coastlines.

4 *TECTARIUS CORONATUS* **Beaded Prickly Winkle** *Valenciennes 1832* (3cm/1¼in) *Indo-Pacific* **A**. A pretty species with nodulose spiral beading in alternate bands of orange and grey. It is found on intertidal rocks.

5 *TECTARIUS PAGODUS* **Pagoda Prickly Winkle** *L. 1758* (5cm/2in) *Indo-Pacific* **C**. A decorative beige-white species with many knobs and protrusions on the whorls. It is found in warmer seas on rocks above the high-water line.

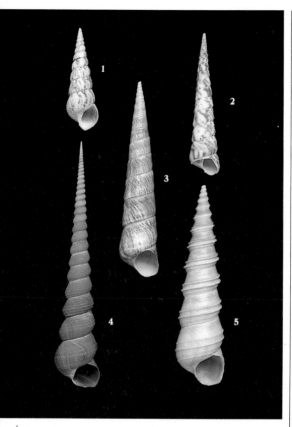

Turritellidae The screw shells number 50–100 species, possibly more. They have tall, pointed spires with many regular whorls. They live in the main in tropical areas on sand and mud in shallow water offshore.

1 *MESALIA OPALINA* **Opal Turritella** *Adams and Reeve 1850* (6cm/2¼in) *W Africa* **U**. A short, squat species with rounded, virtually smooth whorls. The background is a dirty white with fine red-brown wavy axial lines, and the aperture is white.

2 *TURRITELLA RADULA* **Dart Turritella** *Kiener 1843* (10cm/4in) *Gulf of California to Mexico* **U**. This subtidal sand dweller is white, with coarse spiral lirae and vivid red-brown wavy axial lines.

3 *TURRITELLA BRODERIPIANA* **Broderip's Turritella** *Orbigny 1847* (12cm/4¾in) *W Central America* **U**. A tall species with almost straight-sided whorls and fine spiral lirae. The base colour is beige, with flame-like red-brown axial lines.

4 *TURRITELLA TEREBRA* **Screw Shell** *L. 1758* (16cm/6½in) *Indo-Pacific* **A**. An elegant high-spired shell, usually brown to dark brown, which inhabits sandy mud and shallow water.

5 *TURRITELLA DUPLICATA* **Duplicate Turritella** *L. 1758* (12cm/4¾in) *Indo-Pacific* **C**. A species similar in appearance to *Turritella terebra* but has fewer and coarser angled whorls and ribbing. The shell is chunky and heavy and inhabits subtidal sand.

Architectonidae Commonly known as sundials, these shells are all flat and round and have a large umbilicus. They live at a range of depths in tropical seas.

1 *ARCHITECTONICA MAXIMA* **Giant Sundial** *Philippi 1849* (6cm/2¼in) *Indo-Pacific* **C**. A popular shell which inhabits sand at depths of 10–50m (33–165ft). There is a pronounced radial ornamentation of a beige base colour with banding of dark brown squares and dashes.

2 *ARCHITECTONICA NOBILIS* **Noble Sundial** *Röding 1798* (5cm/2in) *Caribbean* **C**. A smaller, paler shell than *Architectonica maxima* and with a body whorl that is more rounded and less angled when seen from the side.

Vermetidae These shells are long, narrow, and coiled, with irregular, often bizarre, shapes resembling worm casts. They grow in groups or live snugly on rocks or other shells.

3 *SILIQUARIA PONDEROSA* **Giant Worm Shell** *Mörch 1860* (to 20cm/8in) *Taiwan to Indo-Pacific* **U**. This shallow-water dweller has whorls which in the early stages are coiled flat but which later grow haphazardly.

4 *SILIQUARIA CUMINGI* **Scaled Worm Shell** *Mörch 1860* (to 20cm/8in) *Taiwan to Philippines* **U**. A long species which has several rows of fine axial lines with slightly protruding scales. The early whorls grow haphazardly, but some then coil in a regular fashion before distorting once again.

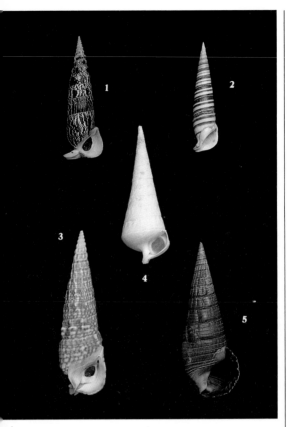

Cerithiidae One of two families of horn snails, the cerithiidae mostly have variable coloration and ornamentation.

1 CERITHIUM CUMINGI **Cummings's Cerith** A. Adams 1855 (8cm/3¼in) Australia **C.** A smooth shell with a cream or white background and black or dark brown spots or blotches and zigzags.

2 RHINOCLAVIS FASCIATA **Striped Cerith** Bruguière 1792 (8cm/3¼in) Australia to Indo-Pacific **C.** A species with variable coloration, but often with spiral banding of black, brown, and cream.

3 PSEUDOVERTAGUS CLAVA **Club Vertagus** Gmelin 1791 (10cm/4in) Polynesia **R.** Found in sand at depths of 20–40m (65–

130ft), this shell is tall and has flat whorls of a cream base colour with fine spiral lines and mottled brown axial lines. The later whorls bear prominent nodules.

Potamididae These shells differ from the ceriths in having the outer lip of the aperture extended and a poorly developed siphonal canal.

4 CAMPANILE SYMBOLICUM **Bell Clapper** Iredale 1917 (15cm/6in) SW Australia **U.** The only species of the genus termed a living fossil, this is a large, chalky white shell.

5 TEREBRALIA PALUSTRIS **Mud Creeper** L. 1767 (12cm/4¾in) Indo-Pacific **C.** A large species, with strong axial ribs, a flaring aperture, and a shiny surface with black axial striae.

Epitoniidae The Epitoniums, or
Wentletraps, are a dainty group
with delicate and attractive rib-
like sculpturing. The name
Wentletrap derives from the
German word for a winding or
spiral staircase, which is an apt
name for most of these shells.
They are mostly pointed and
conical, with whorls adorned with
axial ribbing. The opercula are
corneous and thin, with fine
whorls. There are at least 200
species, most of which inhabit
shallow waters, although some
occur in very deep waters. They
are often found among sea
anemones, on which many feed.
1 *EPITONIUM SCALARE* **Precious
Wentletrap** *L. 1758* (to 6cm/2¼in)
Japan to Philippines **C.** A
wonderfully fascinating shell, this
species has only become common
in the last 30 years or so and is
now fished in large numbers off
Taiwan and the Philippines.
During the last century it was
rarely collected – indeed so rare
was it at one time that it is said
that clever Chinese craftsmen
made counterfeits of rice-flour
paste. The deception was only
discovered when the new owner
washed the specimen, which
would promptly disintegrate.
Stories from the eighteenth and
nineteenth centuries tell of
wealthy people exchanging large
sums of money for the shell.
  The shell is off-white and the
rounded whorls are separated by
prominent axial ribs which hold
the shell together. The operculum
is corneous and black.

1 *STHENORYTIS PERNOBILIS*
Noble Wentletrap *Fischer and
Bernardi 1857* (4cm/1½in)
Caribbean **R**. A much sought after
shell since very few are fished
from its habitat of deep waters of
100–500m (330–4920ft). It is
usually taken in traps or by
crabbers.
2 *CIRSOTREMA VARICOSUM*
Varicose Wentletrap *Lamarck
1822* (4cm/1½in) *Central
Philippines* **C**. A greyish-white
shell with a tall, acute spire with
rounded whorls covered in coarse
axial crenulated striae.
3 *AMAEA FERMINIANA*
Ferminiana Wentletrap *Dall
1908* (4cm/1½in) *W Central
America* **U**. The coloration ranges
from off-white to grey-beige and
there are convex whorls with fine

spiral cords and axial lines that
create a netted appearance. The
shell is fished offshore.
4 *EPITONIUM RUGOSUM Kuroda
and Ito 1961* (to 7cm/2¾in) *Central
Philippines* **R**. A delicate and
beautiful shell, normally white
and with a tall spire of about 12
convex and sharply shouldered
whorls. There are numerous tall,
narrow axial ribs with fine
crenulations.
5 *AMAEA MAGNIFICA*
Magnificent Wentletrap
Sowerby 1844 (to 8cm/3¼in)
Taiwan to Japan **U**. A tall, thin,
and graceful shell and one of the
largest in the family. A collectors'
favourite, it is off-white, with fine
axial cords.

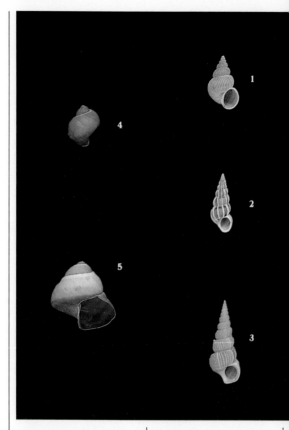

1 *EPITONIUM IMPERIALIS*
Imperial Wentletrap *Sowerby 1844* (2cm/⅘in) *W Australia* **U.** A short, squat species with rounded, convex whorls and fine axial ribs. It is subtidal and found in sand.
2 *EPITONIUM LAMELLOSUM*
Lamellose Wentletrap
Lamarck 1822 (2.5cm/1in) *NE Atlantic and Mediterranean* **C.** The spire is smallish but tall and there are rounded grey whorls with strong, white axial ribs. These are joined at sutures from the apex to the body whorl.
3 *EPITONIUM GUINEENSIS*
Guinea Wentletrap *Bouchet and Tellier 1978* (5cm/2in) *W Africa* **U.** This beige-white shell has a tall spire with about ten whorls and is rounded and convex, with axial and spiral netted striae.

Janthinidae The purple sea snails are thin, fragile shells described as pelagic: they float on the surface of the water on a raft of mucus-covered bubbles. They feed on other floating marine life and are usually found washed up on the shore, but rarely with perfect lips.
4 *JANTHINA GLOBOSA* **Globular Janthina** *Swainson 1822* (2cm/⅘in) *Indo-Pacific* **C.** A rounded shell, with a depressed spire and a large body whorl.
5 *JANTHINA JANTHINA* **Common Purple Snail** *L. 1758* (3.5cm/1⅓in) *Worldwide in tropical seas* **C.** The largest species in the group, this shell has a depressed spire and a large, rounded body whorl with an angled periphery.

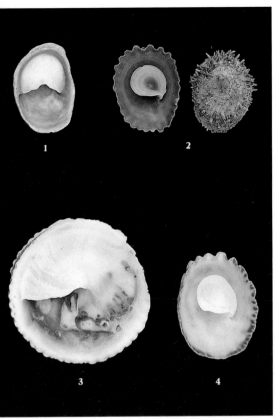

Calyptraeidae Slipper shells are
generally flat, conical, and limpet-
shaped. The surface can be
smooth, ridged, or spiny. Inside
there is a shelf-like structure
under which the soft organs of the
creature are protected. These
species, widely distributed in
most seas of the world, live
mainly on rocks or on other
shelled animals, filter-feeding on
vegetable matter.
1 *CREPIDULA FORNICATA*
Atlantic Slipper *L. 1758*
(4cm/1½in) *E USA and NE
Atlantic* **A**. This species inhabits
rocks in colonies in which one
shell lives on top of another,
forming a chain. The dorsum is a
mottled beige-white, the shoulder
white, and the aperture orange.
2 *CRUCIBULUM SPINOSUM* **Spined**

Cup and Saucer *Sowerby 1824*
(4cm/1½in) *W Central America* **C**.
An oval shell with dorsal margins
which are covered in spines. The
apex area is free of spines but is
usually encrusted. This species
lives on rocks and other shells at
depths down to 50m (165ft).
3 *TROCHITA TROCHIFORMIS*
Rayed Peruvian Hat *Born 1778*
(6cm/2½in) *W South America* **C**.
Found offshore on rocks, this is a
flattened, rounded, and limpet-
like shell. The ridged dorsum is
usually heavily encrusted.
4 *CRUCIBULUM SCUTELLATUM*
Shield Cup and Saucer *Wood
1828* (5cm/2in) *W Central America*
C. A rounded shell with a pink,
brown, or white interior and a
white cup. The exterior is ridged,
with nodules or scales.

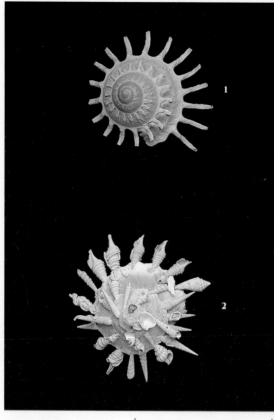

Xenophoridae These form one of the most interesting families in the whole world of shells. The animal, using its foot, picks up dead shells, stones, and other marine debris and cements them with a secretion to the upper side of its own shell. The reason for this is not thought to be to provide camouflage, for there is little or no light at the depths which some of the species inhabit. One theory is that the additional material helps to strengthen an otherwise very thin and fragile shell or prevents it sinking into muddy substrate. Particular species, such as *Xenophora pallidula*, are raised by these attachments 1–1.5cm ($\frac{1}{2}$–$\frac{3}{4}$in) above the seabed on which they live, possibly to allow the free passage of food-carrying water.

1 *STELLARIA SOLARIS* **Sunburst Carrier Shell** *L. 1767* (9cm/3$\frac{1}{2}$in) *Indo-Pacific U.* This thin, pale brown shell is conical, with a low spire and has hollow, ray-like projections at the periphery. It is usually devoid of the attachments found in related species.

2 *XENOPHORA PALLIDULA* **Pale Carrier Shell** *Reeve 1842* (12cm/4$\frac{3}{4}$in) *Philippines and South Africa C.* This is probably the most spectacular member of the family, often bearing many fine and delicate dead shells on its dorsum, although corals and occasionally various species of hard sponge are also found. The original body of the shell is very thin and fragile, with a rounded shape and a low spire.

1 *XENOPHORA CRISPA*
Mediterranean Carrier Shell
Koenig 1831 (5cm/2in) *NE
Atlantic and Mediterranean* **U.**
Occasionally trawled from depths
of 50–80m (165–260ft), this shell
is often found covered with stones
and pebbles. It has an oval, thin,
brown operculum.
2 *TUGURIUM LONGLEYI*
Longley's Carrier Shell
Bartsch 1931 (13cm/5in)
Caribbean **U.** A large, thin species
which seldom has many
attachments. The wide, flattened
body whorl of this deep-water
species is often damaged.
3 *XENOPHORA CEREA* **Rough
Carrier Shell** *Reeve 1843*
(9cm/3½in) *Indo-Pacific* **C.** The
spire, viewed between
attachments, is strongly ridged

and uneven, while the base has
radiating ridges and growth lines.
The species is usually covered
with stones and corals.
4 *XENOPHORA DIGITATA* **Finger
Carrier Shell** *von Marten 1878*
(7cm/2¾in) *W Africa* **U.** The beige-
white shell is normally bare. The
periphery of the body whorl has
short, downward-pointing
projections.
5 *XENOPHORA CONCHYLIOPHORA*
Atlantic Carrier Shell *Born
1780* (8cm/3¼in) *SE USA and
Caribbean* **C.** A shallow-water
shell usually encrusted with coral
fragments, stones, and a few
bivalves. The base and the
dorsum (when seen) are beige-
brown.

Strombidae Most species possess, near the anterior end, a stromboid notch through which a stalked eye protrudes when the creature is moving around or feeding.

The *Lambis* species have a characteristic flaring outer lip with long, finger-like projections or spines, a long siphonal canal, and a pronounced stromboid notch.

1 *TIBIA FUSUS* **Spindle Tibia** *L. 1758* (23cm/9in) *Philippines* **C**. This is a spectacular shell with a tall, slender spire and an equally long and thin straight, or gently curved, siphonal canal. There are five or more finger-like projections on the aperture lip.

2 *TIBIA DELICATULA* **Delicate Tibia** *Nevill 1881* (7cm/2¾in) *Indian Ocean* **U**. A short, stocky, and robust shell with a high spire and a short, pointed canal.

3 *TIBIA MARTINI* **Martin's Tibia** *Marrat 1877* (12cm/4¾in) *Philippines* **C**. This deep-water species has a very thin light-beige shell and a large body whorl.

4 *TIBIA CURTA* **Indian Tibia** *Sowerby 1842* (12cm/4¾in) *Indian Ocean* **C**. A smooth species very similar to *Tibia insulaechorab*, but with a longer and straighter siphonal canal.

5 *TIBIA INSULAECHORAB* **Arabian Tibia** *Röding 1798* (14cm/5½in) *Indian Ocean* **C**. A smooth, rich-brown shell with a tall spire. It has a curved siphonal canal and five short, stumpy projections on the outer edge of the aperture lip.

1 *TEREBELLUM TEREBELLUM*
Little Auger Shell L. *1758*
(4cm/1½in) *Indo-Pacific* **C**. A very
smooth, glossy, and bullet-shaped
shell, with a truncated lip at the
anterior end. Pattern and colour
are highly variable in this subtidal
sand-dwelling species.

2 *TIBIA POWISI* **Powis's Tibia**
Petit 1842 (4cm/1½in) *Japan to
Australia* **U**. A small species with
noticeable spiral ornamentation,
a white aperture with minute
"fingers", and a short canal.

3 *VARICOSPIRA CANCELLATA*
Cancellate Tibia *Lamarck 1822*
(3cm/1½in) *Indo-Pacific* **U**. Fine
axial ribs and spiral grooves give
this shell, which is found in
offshore waters, a cancellate
ornamentation. The canal is very
short.

4 *VARICOSPIRA CRISPATA* **Netted
Tibia** *Sowerby 1842* (2.5cm/1in)
Philippines **U**. Probably the
smallest member of the group,
this shell has prominent axial
ridges with spiral bands of brown
on a cream background. The
aperture lip is thickened and
striated and the canal is short.

1 *LAMBIS CHIRAGRA ARTHRITICA*
Arthritic Spider Conch *Röding
1798* (15cm/6in) *E Africa* **C**. The
species is similar to *Lambis
chiragra*, but smaller and lighter.
The interior lip and columella are
strongly lirate, and the coloration
is white on purple-brown. There
are deep spiral ridges on the body
whorl, which is beige-white with
mottled brown dashes and
blotches. It is commonly found on
coral reefs.
2 *LAMBIS CHIRAGRA* **Chiragra
Spider Conch** *L. 1758* (to
25cm/10in) *Indo-Pacific* **C**. This
inhabitant of shallow water has a
low spire with coarse cords on the
body whorl. There are five strong,
thick spines and the siphonal
canal is curved. The aperture is
pink-orange, the columella are

lirate, and the parietal area is
wide.
3 *LAMBIS TRUNCATA* **Giant
Spider Conch** *Humphrey 1786*
(30cm/12in) *Indo-Pacific* **C**. The
largest member of the genus, this
shell has a depressed spire with a
truncated appearance. This
inhabitant of shallower waters is
off-white to cream and
occasionally orange.

1 *LAMBIS VIOLACEA* **Violet Spider Conch** *Swainson 1821* (10cm/4in) *W Indian Ocean* **R**. Probably the rarest shell of its genus, this deep-water dweller has a vivid purple aperture and 10 or more short lip projections, those at the posterior end slightly longer.

2 *LAMBIS CROCATA CROCATA* **Orange Spider** *Link 1807* (12cm/4¾in) *E Africa to Philippines* **C**. The spire is smallish, the body whorl has long, thin projections, and the aperture in this reef dweller is a deep orange.

3 *LAMBIS SCORPIUS* **Scorpion Spider** *L. 1758* (13cm/5in) *W Pacific* **C**. The interior coloration of this coral-reef dweller is vivid purple, with white transverse striae on the columella and the inner lip. It has irregular, lumpy projections.

4 *LAMBIS DIGITATA* **Finger Spider Conch** *Perry 1811* (12cm/4¾in) *E Africa* **C**. This shallow-water species has a relatively tall spire and a ribbed and knobbed dorsum of a mottled brown. The posterior canal projection bifurcates above the spire.

5 *LAMBIS MILLEPEDA* **Millipede Spider Conch** *L. 1758* (10cm/4in) *W Pacific* **C**. This shallow-water dweller has a spirally ribbed, shortened spire. The aperture is narrow and bears three long spines at the posterior end and six short, curved ones opposite the columella.

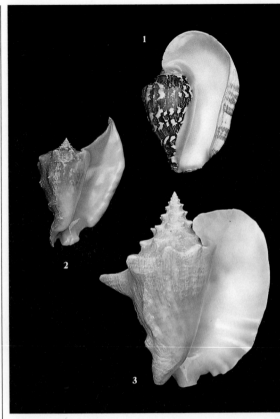

1 *STROMBUS LATISSIMUS* **Wide-mouthed Conch** L. *1758* (15cm/6in) *W Pacific* **U.** The shell is thick and heavy for its size and is often encrusted. The lip is wide and flaring, thickening at the extremities, and the body whorl has rich red-brown markings. Perfect specimens are rare in this species, which dwells in relatively shallow water, most commonly in the Philippines.

2 *STROMBUS PERUVIANUS* **Peruvian Conch** *Swainson 1823* (12cm/4⅜in) *W Central America* **U.** When the animal is alive, the exterior of the shell is covered with a thick brown periostracum which flakes off when dried. The spire is short, the body whorl is large and knobbed, and there is a flaring, thickened lip which extends into a longish curved projection at its posterior end. The stromboid notch is pronounced. This inhabitant of low-tide pools has an interior that ranges from dark orange to pink, often with a metallic tinge.

3 *STROMBUS GIGAS* **Queen** or **Pink Conch** L. *1758* (to 23cm/9in) *Caribbean* **C.** The familiar "conch" is seen at nearly every seaside gift shop. It is a major source of food and occurs abundantly in many West Indian islands, where it lives in shallow water on sand. The species occasionally produces pink pearls and the spire is sometimes removed for use as a crude wind instrument.

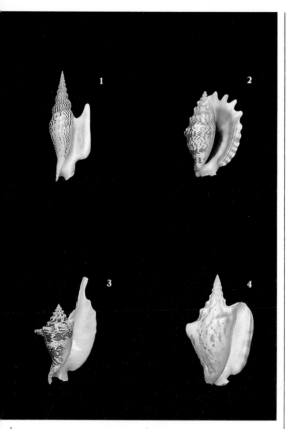

1 *STROMBUS LISTERI* **Lister's Conch** *T. Gray 1852* (12cm/4¾in) *Bay of Bengal* **U**. Once a great rarity, this deep-water dweller is now fished more frequently. The spire is tall and elegant and the lip is thin, flaring, and curves upwards.

2 *STROMBUS SINUATUS* **Laciniate Conch** *Lightfoot 1786* (10cm/4in) *SW Pacific* **C**. This species inhabits coarse coral sandbeds and is common in the Central Philippines. Its aperture is vivid purple and the outer lip has four flattened leaf-like processes at the posterior end.

3 *STROMBUS GALLUS* **Rooster Tail Conch** *L. 1758* (12cm/4¾in) *Caribbean to E South America* **U**. The species is not dissimilar to *Strombus peruvianus*, but is

smaller and has a more angled shoulder on the body whorl and an undulating or frilled outer lip. The posterior end of the lip is pronounced and curved, suggesting a rooster's tail.

4 *STROMBUS THERSITES* **Thersite Stromb** *Swainson 1823* (14cm/5½in) *SW Pacific* **R**. A chunky, thick shell with an extended slender spire and a thickened, flared lip. The exterior coloration is cream-beige and white around the aperture. There is a thick transverse banding of red-brown on white on the lip's inner edge. The species inhabits shallow water offshore.

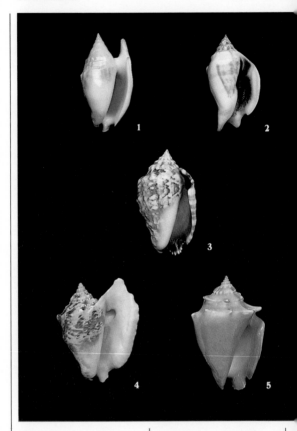

1 *STROMBUS BULLA* **Bubble Conch** *Röding 1798* (5cm/2in) *SW Pacific* **C**. A shallow-water sand dweller, this species has a white interior and a fleshy-red exterior. The spire is callused and there is a short projection at the top of the lip.

2 *STROMBUS KLECKHAMAE* **Kleckham's Conch** *Cernohorsky 1971* (5cm/2in) *Philippines* **R**. Only recently available in any numbers, this shell has a smooth, brown-white exterior and tuberculated whorls. The aperture is black to yellow and lirate and the species has a pronounced notch.

3 *STROMBUS PIPUS* **Butterfly Conch** *Röding 1798* (5cm/2in) *SW Pacific* **C**. The species lives on sand in relatively shallow waters

to a depth of 75m (245ft). The dorsum is coarse and knobbed, the aperture is a deep brown-black, and the columella are white and callused.

4 *STROMBUS RANINUS* **Hawk-wing Conch** *Gmelin 1791* (7cm/2¾in) *Caribbean* **C**. The spire is short and the large body whorl bears two sizeable knobs. The flared lip is slightly frilled and the aperture is pinkish fading to white.

5 *STROMBUS PUGILIS* **West Indian Fighting Conch** *L. 1758* (8cm/3¼in) *Florida and Caribbean* **C**. The name derives from the strong blows of the animal's foot during combat. It lives on sand or grass and has a cream exterior and red-orange columella and aperture.

1 *STROMBUS GIBBERULUS* **Humped Conch** *L. 1758* (5cm/ 2in) *E Africa to Indian Ocean* **C**. A smooth, pear-shaped shell with a short spire. An intertidal dweller, it has a white-rimmed outer lip and a purplish aperture with fine lirae.

2 *STROMBUS MARGINATUS* **Margined Strombus** *L. 1758* (4.5cm/1¾in) *Indian Ocean* **C**. The spire is short and the body whorl is triangular and smooth, with a sharply angled shoulder. There is brown and white spiral patterning and the aperture is white.

3 *STROMBUS VITTATUS VITTATUS* **Turrid Strombus** *L. 1758* (7cm/ 2¾in) *Thailand to W Pacific* **C**. This species lives on mud or sand to a depth of 40m (130ft) and has a slender, pointed spire with axial ribs. The lip is relatively narrow.

4 *STROMBUS PLICATUS SIBBALDI Sowerby 1842* (3cm/1¼in) *Indian Ocean* **C**. The spire is tall and slender and the body whorl is large, with a pustuled shoulder. The aperture of this frequently dredged species is white with fine transverse striae.

5 *STROMBUS FASCIATUS* **Lined Conch** *Born 1778* (4cm/1½in) *Red Sea* **C**. A stout, low-spired shell with knobs on the shoulder of the body whorl. An inhabitant of sand in shallow water.

6 *STROMBUS LUHUANUS* **Blood Conch** *L. 1758* (to 5cm/2in) *W Pacific* **A**. This commercially fished shell is thick and stocky, with a depressed spire. It lives on sand to a depth of 10m (33ft).

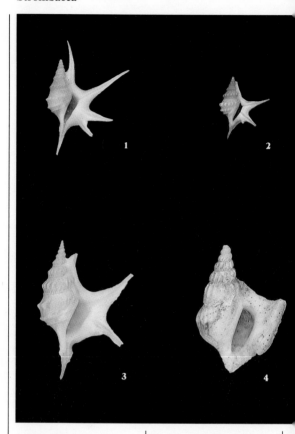

Aporrhaidae The few members of this group are thick but smallish and are found in temperate to cool waters around the world. Their fossil ancestors possessed in many cases very long and bizarre shapes and spines. The outer lip is flattened and has long, pointed projections suggestive of a bird's foot.

1 *A PORRHAIS SERRESIANUS Michaud 1828* (4.5cm/1¾in) *Mediterranean U*. The spire and body whorl are slender in this deep-water dweller. It has spiral beaded cords, two of them on the body whorl. There are three or four long processes, in many cases curved, and a long siphonal canal.

2 *A PORRHAIS SENEGALENSIS* **Senegalese Pelican's Foot** *Gray 1838* (2.5cm/1in) *W Africa*

U. This is possibly the smallest member of the group. It has brown nodulose whorls, a long siphonal canal, and three processes, one of which is commonly alongside the spire.

3 *A PORRHAIS PESPELECANI* **Common Pelican's Foot** *L. 1758* (4cm/1½in) *Mediterranean C*. This species inhabits relatively deep water at depths of 50–175m (165–575ft). It has nodulose whorls, a long siphonal canal, and three calloused "fingers".

4 *A PORRHAIS OCCIDENTALIS* **American Pelican's Foot** *Beck 1836* (4cm/1½in) *E Canada and USA U*. A deep-water dweller with a dirty-white-brown coloration and a wide, flaring lip. It lacks the sharp processes of other species in the group.

Cypraeidae The cowries are probably more popular than any other group of shells and total over 200 species. They are generally oval in shape and possess a high, smooth, glossy surface which is usually highly coloured and patterned. This appearance is created by the animal's mantle, which extends over the shell from both sides and is often as colourful as the shell itself. The apertures on the underside are fairly narrow and most species possess rows of teeth on both the inner (columellar) and outer lips. Cowries feed on coral polyps, soft corals, and detritus.
1 *CYPRAEA AURANTIUM* **Golden Cowrie** *Gmelin 1791* (9cm/3½in) *Philippines to Fiji and Solomons* **R**. One of the two most sought-after of all shells (the other is *Conus gloria-maris*), this species was first observed during the early voyages to the South Pacific, where it was worn as status symbol and adornment.

The shell is still generally regarded as rare. Even rarer are the so-called "gem" specimens. These are unlikely to decrease in value in the foreseeable future. It is probable, however, that the populations of this species are quite large in the areas of habitat and that local dealers and fishermen let them on to the market very slowly, to avoid any hint of a glut. At the time of writing you should expect to pay £200–300 ($350–500) for a prime specimen. It inhabits reef caves or holes about 20m (65ft) deep.

57

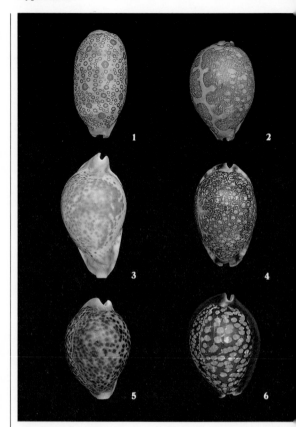

1 *CYPRAEA ARGUS* **Eyed Cowrie**
L. 1758 (7cm/2¾in) *SW Pacific* *C*.
This coral-reef dweller is
cylindrical and has a beige
coloration with rings and blotches
of a darker brown.
2 *CYPRAEA MAPPA* **Map Cowrie**
L. 1758 (7cm/2¾in) *Indo-Pacific* *C*.
A handsome cylindrical or ovate
species with a pink or beige
ground coloration with
reticulated brown markings
resembling contour lines on a
map. It is found mainly on reefs.
3 *CYPRAEA HESITATA*
Umbilicate Cowrie *Iredale 1916*
(9cm/3½in) *SE Australia* *C*. A
largish pyriform shell with a
flattened base and a sunken spire.
The anterior canal is extended
and the posterior canal is curved.
It is an offshore species.

4 *CYPRAEA ARABICA IMMANIS*
Giant Arabian Cowrie *Schilder
and Schilder 1939* (to 10cm/4in)
SE Africa *C*. The largest species of
the arabica complex, this shell has
thickened, callused margins and
brown lines and reticulations on a
pale-green-beige background.
5 *CYPRAEA PANTHERINA*
Panther Cowrie *Lightfoot 1786*
(to 8cm/3¼in) *Red Sea* *C*. The
coloration varies widely from
near-albino to dark-red-black,
although the shape remains
constant.
6 *CYPRAEA MAURITIANA* **Hump-
backed Cowrie** *L. 1758* (8cm/
3¼in) *Indo-Pacific* *C*. This species
is large and a rich brown-black
and has thickened margins and a
humped dorsum. It lives under
rocks.

1 *CYPRAEA CAMELOPARDALIS*
Camel Cowrie *Perry 1811* (6cm/
2¼in) *Red Sea U*. The base,
margins, and extremities of this
offshore species are off-white and
it has coarse black teeth. The
dorsum is pink-beige with small
white spots.
2 *CYPRAEA CERVINETTA*
Panamanian Deer Cowrie
Kiener 1843 (8cm/3¼in) *W Central
America C*. A cylindrical, flattish
cowrie with pronounced
extremities, this shell is found at
low tide and is generally brown-
grey with pale lavender tints and
white spots and blotches.
3 *CYPRAEA STERCORARIA* **Rat
Cowrie** *L. 1758* (8cm/3¼in) *W
Africa C*. This species varies in
shape, but is generally thick and
has a steeply humped dorsum. It

lives under rocks in shallow
water. Dwarf shells occur, with a
mature size of 3–4cm (1¼–1½in).
4 *CYPRAEA TIGRIS* **Tiger Cowrie**
L. 1758 (10cm/4in) *Indo-Pacific
A*. The best known of all cowries,
this shell varies in both size and
colour, but invariably has spots
and blotches on the variable
ground colour. A giant form from
Hawaii grows to 14cm (5½in).
5 *CYPRAEA TALPA* **Mole Cowrie**
L. 1758 (to 8cm/3¼in) *Indo-Pacific
C*. This inhabitant of intertidal
coral reefs has rich brown-black
margins and extremities and
broad brown dorsal bands on a
cream-yellow background. It has
fine teeth.

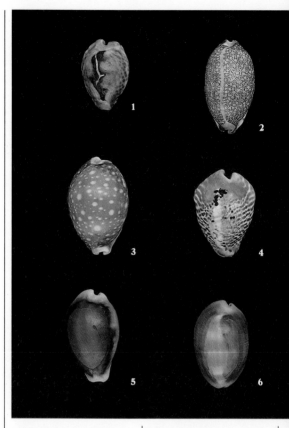

1 *CYPRAEA TEULEREI* **Teulère's Cowrie** *Cazanavette 1845* (5cm/2in) *Gulf of Oman C*. This attractive shell with unusual markings was virtually unknown until the late 1960s, when Oman's reefs were explored by British airmen. It became common within two or three years.

2 *CYPRAEA EGLANTINA* **Eglantine Cowrie** *Duclos 1833* (6cm/2¼in) *Indo-Pacific C*. This inhabitant of coral reefs is cylindrical and has an overall pale-beige-green coloration with a fine netting pattern over it.

3 *CYPRAEA VITELLUS* **Pacific Deer Cowrie** *L. 1758* (6cm/2¼in) *Indo-Pacific C*. The shell is ovate and has a cream-white base and a fawn-to-brown dorsum with white spots and blotches. It lives

under stones and corals.

4 *CYPRAEA MUS DONMOOREI* **Don Moore's Cowrie** *Petuch 1979* (5cm/2in) *Venezuela U*. A larger, heavier variant of the more common Mouse Cowrie, this species lives in relatively shallow water to a depth of 50m (165ft).

5 *CYPRAEA SPADICEA* **Chestnut Cowrie** *Swainson 1823* (6cm/2¼in) *California C*. A handsome, pyriform species with a rich-brown dorsum edged with irregular patches of a darker brown. It is found on or under rock ledges.

6 *CYPRAEA VENTRICULUS* **Ventriculate Cowrie** *Lamarck 1810* (5cm/2in) *Central Pacific U*. This attractive species inhabits coral reefs and is a rich orange-brown with a paler dorsum.

1 *CYPRAEA EROSA* **Eroded
Cowrie** L. *1758* (3.5cm/1¼in)
Indo-Pacific **A**. A smallish but
robust species that inhabits reefs.
It is ovate and the margins are
thickened and pitted, with a
brown blotch either side
spreading to the base. The teeth
are coarse.

2 *CYPRAEA PULCHRA* **Lovely
Cowrie** Gray *1824* (to 5cm/2in)
Red Sea to Gulf of Oman **U**. A
cylindrical shell with a very glossy
surface and a fawn-beige
coloration with two black spots at
each end. There are three broad,
brownish transverse bands on the
dorsum. It lives in corals.

3 *CYPRAEA TURDUS* **Thrush
Cowrie** Lamarck *1810* (4cm/1½in)
Red Sea to W Indian Ocean **C**.
Ovate and somewhat flattened,

this species varies in size and has a
pale-beige-green, spotted dorsum.
The margins are thickened and
grey with large spots and
blotches. The teeth are short.

4 *CYPRAEA LYNX* **Lynx Cowrie**
L. *1758* (to 6cm/2¼in) *Indo-Pacific*
A. A well-known cowrie which
inhabits coral reefs. It is ovate,
has deeply incised orange teeth on
a white base, and has a cream-
orange (occasionally with a bluish
tint) dorsum with many blotches.
There is a distinct dorsal line.

5 *CYPRAEA NIVOSA* **Cloudy
Cowrie** Broderip *1837* (5cm/2in)
Andaman Sea **U**. At one time a
rarity, this shell is now often
taken off Thailand. It is grey-
beige with paler blotches and
spots and has a distinct dorsal
line.

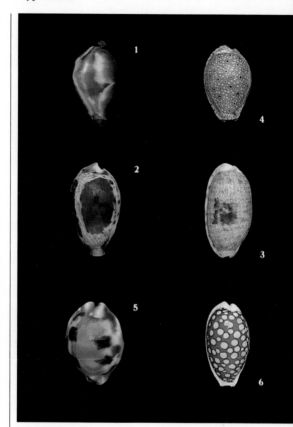

1 *CYPRAEA ONYX* **Onyx Cowrie**
L. 1758 (3.5cm/1¼in) *Indo-Pacific*
C. A very beautiful reef-dwelling
species which is pyriform. It has a
deep-brown-black base and
margins.
2 *CYPRAEA PULCHELLA*
Beautiful Cowrie *Swainson*
1823 (4cm/1½in) *W Pacific* **U.**
Dredged from depths of 30–80m
(100–395ft), this attractive
pyriform shell has one or more
large, rich-brown dorsal blotches
on a beige-green background and
strong, dark-brown teeth.
3 *CYPRAEA TERES* **Tapering**
Cowrie *Gmelin 1791* (4cm/1½in)
Indo-Pacific **C.** Variable in shape,
the shell has a base colour of blue-
grey mottled with green-brown
dots and blotches, usually in
transverse bands.

4 *CYPRAEA OCELLATA* **Ocellated**
Cowrie *L. 1758* (2.5cm/1in)
Indian Ocean **C.** This ovate shell
has short, coarse teeth and lives
among stones and mud in the low-
tide zone.
5 *CYPRAEA TESSELLATA*
Checkerboard Cowrie
Swainson 1822 (3.5cm/1¼in)
Hawaii **R.** A much sought-after
species on account of its
distinctive pattern and
coloration. It lives in and under
coral ledges to a depth of 40m
(130ft).
6 *CYPRAEA CRIBRARIA* **Sieve**
Cowrie *L. 1758* (3cm/1¼in) *Indo-*
Pacific **C.** The shell is generally
ovate, light, and is a distinctive
pale orange-brown with near-
circular dots on the dorsum.
Several subspecies occur.

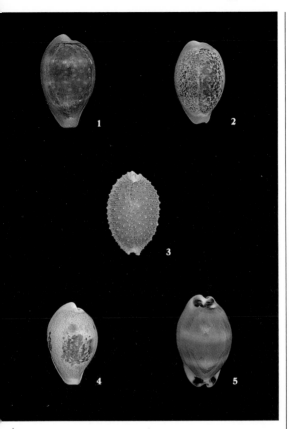

1 *CYPRAEA PYRUM* **Pear Cowrie**
Gmelin 1791 (4cm/1½in) *NW
Africa to Mediterranean C.* The
shell is pyriform and has a rich
orange-red base and margins,
while the dorsum is a mottled
brown with wide cream
transverse bands. It is found
offshore to a depth of 50m (165ft).
2 *CYPRAEA ACHATIDEA* **Agate
Cowrie** *Sowerby 1837* (4cm/1½in)
NW Africa to E Mediterranean R.
The rarest of the Mediterranean
cowries, this species is inflated
and pyriform, and is generally
lightweight.
3 *CYPRAEA GRANULATA*
Granulated Cowrie *Pease 1862*
(3.5cm/1½in) *Hawaii U.* In its
adult form this is the only non-
glossy cowrie. It is ovate, has a
flat dorsum covered with pinkish

pustules on a beige-pink
background, and has strong teeth
to the margins. It is found at
depths of 1–7m (3–23ft) on corals.
4 *CYPRAEA SUBVIRIDIS* **Green-
tinted Cowrie** *Reeve 1835*
(3cm/1½in) *Australia C.* Found
among coral or under rocks, this
shell is inflated and pyriform,
with a pale-green-beige coloration
and a central square or blotches of
dark brown on the dorsum.
5 *CYPRAEA LURIDA* **Lurid
Cowrie** *L. 1758* (4cm/1½in) *NW
Africa to Mediterranean C.* An
ovate, lightweight, and inflated
shell which inhabits shallow
water. It is brown-beige with two
pale transverse dorsal bands and
each of the extremities has two
dark blotches.

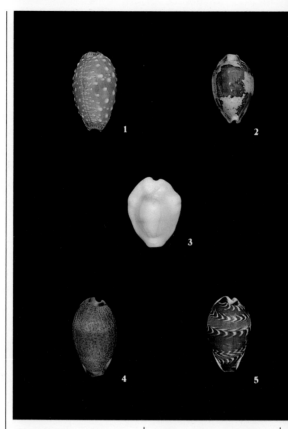

1 *CYPRAEA LIMACINA Lamarck 1810* (3cm/1¼in) *E Africa to W Pacific C.* A species that is variable in its sculpturing – the dorsum may or may not possess nodules. Fresh shells are almost black and fade to slate grey with white spots or nodules. It is found among corals and stones on reefs.

2 *CYPRAEA STOLIDA* **Stolid Cowrie** *L. 1758* (3cm/1¼in) *W Pacific C.* A species which varies in shape from ovate to cylindrical and has distinctive dorsal blotches of a deep-red-brown. It is found on reefs under stones and on coral heads. There are several subspecies and variations.

3 *CYPRAEA MONETA* **Money Cowrie** *L. 1758* (3cm/1¼in) *Indo-Pacific A.* Variable in size and ranging in colour from white to deep orange, this shell was used as currency until recently by the natives of tropical areas. It is found under stones and on rocks in shallow water.

4 *CYPRAEA XANTHODON* **Yellow-toothed Cowrie** *Sowerby 1832* (3cm/1¼in) *Australia C.* A one-time rarity, this shell is now commonly found off northern and eastern Queensland in shallow reef areas.

5 *CYPRAEA DILUCULUM* **Dawn Cowrie** *Reeve 1845* (2.5cm/1in) *E Africa C.* Spectacular markings make this a popular shell with collectors. It is found in shallow water among corals and stones. The inhabitant is jet black.

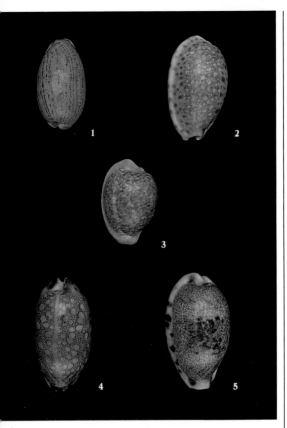

1 *CYPRAEA ISABELLA* **Isabelline Cowrie** *L. 1758* (to 4cm/1½in) *Indo-Pacific* **C**. A generally long and cylindrical species which lives in shallow water. The extremities are tipped with orange, there are very fine axial lines and dashes on the dorsum, and the base is white. There are several variants.

2 *CYPRAEA CHINENSIS* **Chinese Cowrie** *Gmelin 1791* (4cm/1½in) *E Africa to W Pacific* **C**. This species inhabits water ranging from shallow to deep, depending on the location. It has a yellow-green ringed and blotched dorsum, lilac spotting on the margins, and orange-red teeth.

3 *CYPRAEA FUSCORUBRA Shaw 1909* (3cm/1½in) *Cape Province, South Africa* **R**. Comparatively rare until collecting by scuba

divers became popular in recent years, this shell is found at depths of 20–50m (65–165ft).

4 *CYPRAEA SCURRA* **Jester Cowrie** *Gmelin 1791* (4cm/1½in) *Indo-Pacific* **C**. This is the smallest, most elongate, and most cylindrical species in the arabica group. The base colour is pale-green-beige and there are fine rings and a netting of brown on the dorsum. The teeth are short and reddish.

5 *CYPRAEA CAURICA* **Caurica Cowrie** *L. 1758* (to 4cm/1½in) *Indo-Pacific* **A**. Extremely variable in shape and pattern, this shallow-water species is widespread and has many variants. It is generally ovate to cylindrical, and is thick and heavy, with coarse teeth.

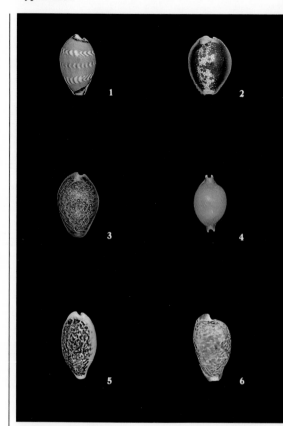

1 *C YPRAEA ZICZAC* **Zigzag Cowrie** *Lamarck 1810* (2cm/¾in) *E Africa to W Pacific* **C**. This small, ovate shell is orange-light-brown overlaid with transverse zigzag bands. It mainly inhabits corals in shallow water.

2 *C YPRAEA HELVOLA* **Honey Cowrie** *L. 1758* (2.5cm/1in) *Indo-Pacific* **C**. This shell is found in coral and has several variants. The base is orange, the margins are deep-red-brown, and the dorsum is mottled.

3 *C YPRAEA ALBUGINOSA* *Gray 1825* (2.5cm/1in) *W Central America* **U**. The coloration is generally pale-pink-mauve with spots and rings of white edged in brown. The teeth are fine. A shallow-water dweller.

4 *C YPRAEA GLOBULUS* **Globose Cowrie** *L. 1758* (to 2.5cm/1in) *Indo-Pacific* **C**. A small, humped, and very smooth shallow-water species with a deep-orange coloration. Both the anterior and posterior canals are extended.

5 *C YPRAEA COXENI* **Cox's Cowrie** *Cox 1873* (3cm/1¼in) *Solomon Islands* **C**. This species was relatively rare until the 1960s. It is ovate and has a distinctive mottled brown dorsum and cream margins and base. It inhabits shallow water on reefs.

6 *C YPRAEA EDENTULA* **Toothless Cowrie** *Gray 1825* (2.5cm/1in) *South Africa* **U**. A pyriform shell with brown mottling on a beige background and extended margins at the posterior end. It has no teeth.

1 *CYPRAEA ENGLERTI* **Father Englert's Cowrie** *Summers and Burgess 1965* (2.5cm/1in) *Easter Island* **R**. A species endemic to Easter Island and named after a local missionary, this shell was very rare until 15–20 years ago. It is found on reefs in relatively shallow water.
2 *CYPRAEA ARABICA DEPRESSA Gray 1824* (4cm/1½in) *Indo-Pacific* **C**. A short, almost rounded shell which has thickened margins. It lives under coral slabs and stones.
3 *CYPRAEA ASELLUS L. 1758* (2cm/⅜in) *Indo-Pacific* **C**. The shell is small and white, with three stark transverse bands of dark-brown-black on the dorsum. It lives on coral reefs.
4 *CYPRAEA LAMARCKII* **Lamarck's Cowrie** *Gray 1825*

(to 5cm/2in) *Indian Ocean* **C**. A handsome ovate and humped species which lives in shallow water on mud. The ground colour is mustard yellow and there are odd spots with a bluish hue.
5 *CYPRAEA EBURNEA* **Pure White Cowrie** *Barnes 1824* (4cm/1½in) *Solomon Islands to New Guinea* **U**. The only naturally all-white cowrie, this shell's range is restricted to the islands east of Australia, where it inhabits coral reefs.

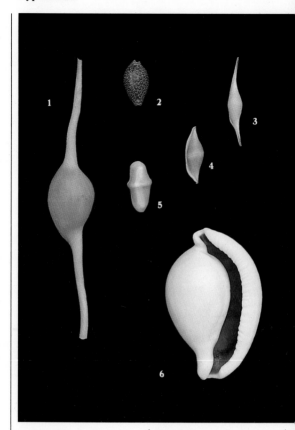

Ovulidae The false cowries are related to the true cowries and include the families Eratoidae and Lamellariidae.

1 *VOLVA VOLVA* **Shuttle Shell** *L. 1758* (12cm/4¾in) *Indo-Pacific* **C**. This fantastically shaped shell has a rounded body whorl and long, slightly curved canals. It is found on coral reefs.

2 *JENNARIA PUSTULATA* *Lightfoot 1786* (2cm/⅞in) *W Central America* **C**. Often mistaken for a true cowrie, this shell is ovate and thick and has an overall grey-blue coloration with many deep-red pustules. It has coarse teeth to the margins.

3 *VOLVA LONGIROSTRATA* *Sowerby 1828* (5cm/2in) *Japan to Philippines* **U**. A very fine and delicate shell with long, curved

posterior and anterior canals. The thin shell is almost transparent.

4 *VOLVA SOWERBYANA* **Sowerby's Shuttle** *Weinkauff 1881* (3cm/1¼in) *Philippines* **U**. A short, fusiform shell with a large oval body whorl extending to shortened, sharp canal extremities, which are usually orange.

5 *CYPHOMA GIBBOSUM* **Flamingo's Tongue** *L. 1758* (2.5cm/1in) *Caribbean* **C**. A cylindrical shell with rounded extremities, this species lives on soft corals. It has a raised central transverse ridge.

6 *OVULA OVUM* **Egg Cowrie** *L. 1758* (10cm/4in) *Indo-Pacific* **C**. A pure white shell with a thickened and ridged lip and an extended posterior canal.

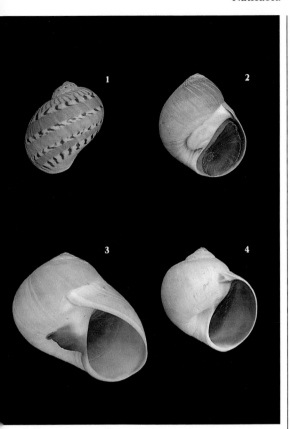

Naticidae Commonly known as necklace shells, the naticidae are rounded with a depressed spire and an enlarged body whorl which is usually smooth and shiny. The foot is used for digging in sand for prey, other molluscs. These species are found in all seas.
1 *NATICA CANRENA* **Colourful Atlantic Moon** *L. 1758* (5cm/2in) *Caribbean* **C.** Found offshore to a depth of 50m (165ft), this shell is brown-beige with spiral banding mixed with zigzag lines and blotches of dark brown. The umbilicus is deep. The lips are seldom perfect.
2 *NEVERITA RECLUSIANA Deshayes 1839* (6cm/2½in) *California to Mexico* **C.** A robust inhabitant of mud in shallow water, this shell is pale beige and has a spire that is slightly raised. It is covered in concentric growth lines and the umbilicus is heavily callused.
3 *NEVERITA DUPLICATA* **Shark Eye** *Say 1822* (to 8cm/3¼in) *SE USA to Caribbean* **C.** A shallow-water dweller on sand, this species is one of the largest of the group. It is beige-brown and has a callused umbilicus and a horny operculum. The depressed tip of the apex suggests the eye of its name.
4 *EUSPIRA HEROS* **Northern Moon** *Say 1822* (9cm/3½in) *NE USA* **C.** A large, chalky-beige species which lives in offshore sand between Newfoundland and the Carolinas.

1 *POLINICES AURANTIUS* **Golden Moon** *Röding 1798* (4cm/1½in) *SW Pacific C.* This shell is somewhat ovate and its coloration is entirely bright orange. By contrast, the callused umbilicus is white.

2 *NATICA LINEATA* **Lined Moon** *Röding 1798* (4cm/1½in) *W Pacific C.* The species lives in sand or mud in relatively shallow water and has axial wavy lines in red-brown on a white background.

3 *POLINICES CONICUS* **Conical Moon** *Lamarck 1822* (to 4cm/1½in) *Australia C.* This intertidal dweller has a relatively high spire which is slightly grey. The body whorl is beige-brown and the aperture dark brown. The umbilicus is deep.

4 *NEVERITA PESELEPHANTI* **Elephant's Foot Moon** *Link*

1807 (4cm/1½in) *Indo-Pacific C.* The species is globulate, with a depressed spire, a callused umbilicus and a thin, corneous operculum. The overall coloration is white, with areas of brown, yellow, or orange covering the body whorl. This species is found in sand in shallow water.

5 *NATICA CRUENTATA* **Hebrew Moon** *Gmelin 1791* (4.5cm/1¾in) *NE Atlantic to Mediterranean C.* This shallow-water species is very variable in pattern, with some examples being spotted, others netted or blotched, and others having wavy lines or other variations.

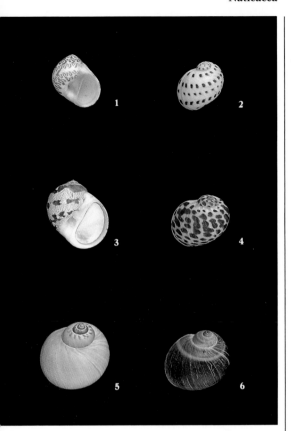

1 *NATICA VIOLACEA* **Violet Moon**
Sowerby 1825 (to 2cm/⅜in) *Indo-Pacific* **U**. A pretty little white
shell with broken spiral bands of
red-brown. The umbilicus of this
shallow-water dweller is lavender
or violet.

2 *NATICA ONCA* **China Moon**
Röding 1798 (to 2.5cm/1¼in) *Indo-Pacific* **C**. A small pure-white
shell with broken spots or
blotches of brown. It lives in
sandy shallow waters.

3 *NATICA FULMINEA* **Lightning
Moon** *Gmelin 1791* (3cm/1⅛in) *W
Africa* **C**. The shell has an off-white background which is
covered with tiny brown dots and
two or three rows of wide, broken
brown dashes or blotches. It has a
white porcellaneous operculum.

4 *NATICA ACINONYX* **African**

Berry Moon *Marche-Marchad
1957* (2.5cm/1in) *W Africa* **R**. This
species, fished from deep water, is
difficult to obtain. It is beige-white with large brown dots and
blotches and a sculptured
calcareous operculum.

5 *NATICA CATENA* **Necklace
Moon** *da Costa 1778* (3.5cm/1¼in)
NE Atlantic to Mediterranean **C**.
There is usually a little decoration
around the early whorls, but
otherwise the shell is an overall
beige-yellow. It lives in sand in
shallow water.

6 *NATICA UNIFASCIATA* **Single-banded Moon** *Lamarck 1822*
(3cm/1⅛in) *Central America* **C**. The
base colour of this shallow-water
species is blue-grey and there is a
cream-yellow spiral band on the
upper part of the body whorl.

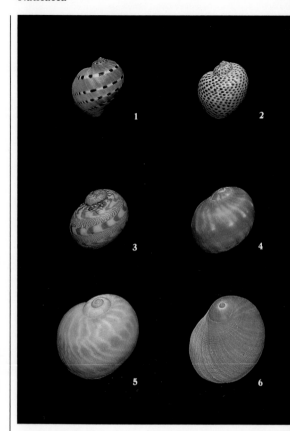

1 *NATICA ALAPAPILIONIS*
Butterfly Moon *Röding 1798* (to
3cm/1¼in) *Indo-Pacific C.* A
prettily marked shell with a beige-
cream background with three or
more white spiral bands blotched
with brown. This sand dweller has
an ornate calcareous operculum.
2 *NATICA FANEL* **Fanel Moon**
Röding 1798 (2.5cm/1in) *W Africa
C.* This species has a depressed
spire, a large, slightly humped
body whorl, and a deep
umbilicus.
3 *TANEA EUZONA Récluz 1844* (to
3cm/1¼in) *Indo-Pacific U.* This
attractive shell inhabits sand at
depths down to 60m (195ft). It is
orange-beige with broad spiral
bands of broken, wavy white. The
calloused umbilicus is white.
4 *NATICA STELLATA* **Starry**

Moon *Hedley 1913* (3.5cm/1⅜in)
W Pacific C. Found in shallow
water in sand, this shell is globose
and is overall orange with axial
banding of deep orange. The
umbilicus is deep.
5 *GLOBULARIA FLUCTUATA* **Wavy
Moon** *Sowerby 1825* (4.5cm/1¾in)
Philippines U. A relatively
popular offshore species with
distinctive decoration, this shell
has a depressed spire, a large body
whorl, and a gaping, extended
aperture.
6 *SINUM CYMBA* **Boat Ear Moon**
Menke 1828 (to 5cm/2in) *W South
America C.* A dweller in shallow,
cool water, this species has fine
concentric growth lines which
contrast strikingly with the
smooth brown interior. The spire
is depressed.

Cassidae Helmet shells are fairly large and solid, with large body whorls and depressed spires. The aperture is generally narrow and has a thickened, toothed outer lip. The columella is enlarged, providing in most cases a wide, thick parietal-shield area. Many species bear blunt tubercules and varices. These shells are mainly inhabitants of sandy areas in warm seas. Members of the genus Phalium are commonly referred to as "bonnets" and are generally thinner and lighter.

1 *CASSIS MADAGASCARIENSIS*
Queen Helmet *Lamarck 1822*
(16cm/6¼in) *Caribbean* **U**. Of medium size and rather lighter than *Cassis tuberosa*, this shallow-water dweller is beige and has a depressed spire and an enlarged body whorl with spiral cords and ridges, some with blunted knobs.

2 *CYPRAECASSIS RUFA*
Bullmouth Helmet *L. 1758*
(15cm/6in) *E Africa* **C**. The so-called "cameo shell" from which popular articles of jewellery are fashioned. It is a thick shell and more ovate than the preceding Cassidae species.

3 *CASSIS TUBEROSA* **King Helmet** *L. 1758* (15cm/6in) *Caribbean* **C**. A medium-sized shallow-water species which is thick and heavy. The triangular, thickened, and smooth outer lip and parietal shield are cream in colour with a dark-brown stain on the columella. The columella and lip bear coarse teeth.

1 *PHALIUM KURODAI* **Kuroda's Bonnet** *Abbott 1968* (6cm/2¼in) *Japan to Australia* **R**. A delicate deep-water species which has blunt nodules on the spire and the body whorl.

2 *CASMARIA ERINACEUS VIBEX* **Vibex Bonnet** *L. 1758* (6cm/2¼in) *Indo-Pacific* **C**. A shallow-water dweller which is variable in size and pattern. Generally the spire is not very depressed and the coloration is beige with brown zigzag axial lines.

3 *PHALIUM THOMSONI* *Brazier 1875* (6cm/2¼in) *S Australia* **U**. A lightweight shell with a relatively high spire. It is off-white with rows of dull, square, brown spots and there are dark-brown markings on the lip.

4 *CASSIS FIMBRIATA* *Quoy and Gaimard 1833* (7cm/2⅜in) *Australia* **U**. A species of the intertidal zone and deep water, this shell is grey-brown with two or three rows of knobs on the body whorl.

5 *PHALIUM FIMBRIA* **Fimbriate Bonnet** *Gmelin 1791* (to 8cm/3¼in) *Indian Ocean* **R**. This is a sought-after species with a limited range. It has a short, pointed spire and an ovate body whorl with convex axial ribs which are pointed at the shoulder.

6 *PHALIUM AREOLA* **Checkered Bonnet** *L. 1875* (7cm/2⅜in) *Indo-Pacific* **C**. Found on mud or sand in shallow water, this shell is smooth and has a beige-grey ground colour with broad spiral bands of squarish brown spots. The spire is depressed.

1 *GALEODEA RUGOSA* **Rugose
Bonnet** *L. 1758* (6cm/2¼in)
Mediterranean **C**. This species has
a habitat which ranges from the
offshore area to deep water. It is a
light shell with fine spiral cords
and a few blunt knobs on the
shoulder.
2 *PHALIUM GRANULATUM* **Ridged
Bonnet** *Gmelin 1791* (9cm/3½in)
Mediterranean **C**. This offshore
dweller is stout and has coarse
spiral bands.
3 *PHALIUM BANDATUM* **Banded
Bonnet** *Perry 1811* (10cm/4in) *W
Pacific* **C**. A large, handsome
Cassis, smooth and with broad,
spiral, alternating bands of cream
and pale brown. This shell
inhabits both shallow and deeper
waters.
4 *PHALIUM STRIGATUM* **Striped

Bonnet** *Gmelin 1791* (to
9cm/3½in) *Japan and Taiwan* **C**.
A popular shell with a smooth,
glossy surface which is beige with
broad, wavy, brown axial lines.
There are distinct varices.
5 *PHALIUM WYVILLEI Watson
1886* (10cm/4in) *Japan to
Australia* **R**. The shell is dredged
in very deep water, sometimes
from depths greater than 450m
(1475ft). It is a thin, light shell,
with very fine spiral cords and
regular, rounded knobs on the
shoulder.
6 *PHALIUM GLAUCUM* **Grey
Bonnet** *L. 1758* (10cm/4in) *Indo-
Pacific* **C**. A thick, solid shell with
a blue-grey coloration. The
thickened, recurved lip is cream
and there are short spines at its
anterior end.

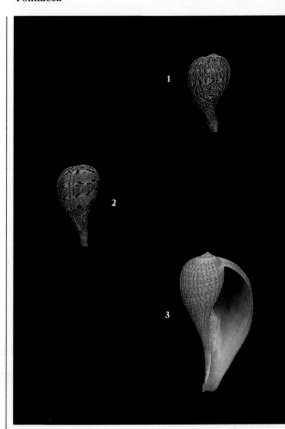

Ficidae A small family of only
one genus, the ficidae are very
thin, light shells with a fig-like
shape and no operculum. They
possess a long siphon and the
mantle lobes cover the shell.
These species inhabit sand in
relatively deep, warm seas.
1 *FICUS VARIEGATA Röding 1798*
(8cm/3¼in) *Japan to Taiwan* **C**.
Shorter and wider than *Ficus
gracilis*, this shallow-water species
has a wide, gaping aperture and a
purplish interior. It is a beige-
brown with darker axial
markings.
2 *FICUS SUBINTERMEDIA*
Underlined Fig *Orbigny 1852*
(10cm/4in) *Indo-Pacific* **C**. A
sturdy shell with raised spiral
cords and fine axial lines. It is pale
brown with cream spiral bands on
which are dark-brown blotches. It
lives offshore in sandy mud.
3 *FICUS GRACILIS* **Graceful Fig**
Sowerby 1825 (13cm/5in) *Japan to
Taiwan* **C**. The largest member of
the group, this shell is a sand
dweller in deeper waters. It has a
depressed spire and fine spiral and
axial cords, and there is a slight
brown mottling on the base
colour of a paler brown.

Tonnidae The Tuns are a small family of rather thin, light shells with depressed spires and somewhat inflated or globose body whorls. There is spiral ornamentation and the siphonal canal is usually deep.

1 *MALEA RINGENS* **Grinning Tun** *Swainson 1822* (15cm/6in) *W Central America* **U**. A solid, heavy, beige-white shell with coarse spiral ribbing, found under rocks or on sand. It has a deeply incised columellar notch and a thickened outer lip with strong, teeth-like folds towards the aperture.

2 *TONNA LUTEOSTOMA* **Gold-mouthed Tun** *Küster 1857* (12cm/4¾in) *W Pacific* **U**. This rounded and rather heavy shell lives in shallow to deep water and has beige-white markings and prominent spiral ribs.

3 *TONNA TESSELLATA* **Tessellated Tun** *Lamarck 1816* (12cm/4¾in) *W Pacific* **C**. The coloration of this species is off-white with raised spiral bands of broken brown-white dashes.

4 *TONNA OLEARIUM L. 1758* (to 20cm/8in) *W Pacific* **C**. A large species, although very thin and light. This shell has an overall dark-brown coloration with a white aperture. There are prominent spiral ribs. The shell may be a variant of *Tonna galea*.

5 *TONNA PERDIX* **Partridge Tun** *L. 1758* (12cm/4¾in) *Indo-Pacific* **C**. This shell lives in offshore sand and is narrow with a fairly high spire and has flat, spiral ribs with shallow grooves between them.

Ranellidae The Tritons are variable in shape and sculpturing and are in many cases covered with a thick periostracum which is often hairy. They also have prominent varices. These species inhabit mainly tropical seas, in either shallow or deep water, where they live on echinoids and other molluscs.

1 *CHARONIA SAULIAE* **Saul's Triton** *Reeve 1844* (17cm/6¾in) *Japan to Taiwan C.* The ground colour is white and there are broad bands of broken brown-beige. The aperture is white with broad brown spiral ribs on the inner edge. This dweller in relatively shallow water has low knobs on the shoulder.

2 *CHARONIA TRITONIS* **Triton Trumpet** *L. 1758* (to 40cm/16in)

Indo-Pacific C. A well-known cornucopia-shaped shell found in shallow water on reefs. The spire is tall and elegant and there are coarse spiral cords and sharp varices. The lip edge has a spirally ribbed interior and the margin is scalloped. This shell has a vivid orange interior and prominent black lirate columella.

3 *CHARONIA VARIEGATA* **Atlantic Triton** *Lamarck 1816* (to 30cm/12in) *S USA and NE Brazil C.* This species is somewhat thicker and heavier than *Charonia tritonis* and its spire rather shorter. The patterning is similar in the two species, but this species occasionally has pink or orange undertones. The shoulder and whorls are sometimes irregular and swollen.

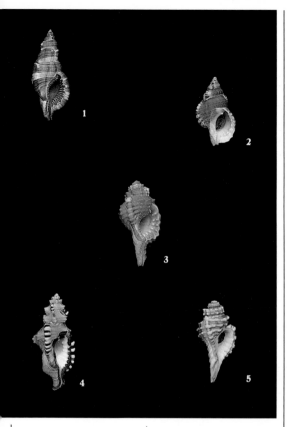

1 *CYMATIUM PILEARE* **Hairy Triton** *L. 1758* (to 9cm/3½in) *Indo-Pacific C.* A shallow-water dweller so-named because the periostracum is covered in short, coarse hairs. It has fine spiral bands and the aperture is deep-red-orange.

2 *MAYENA AUSTRALASIAE* **Australian Triton** *Perry 1811* (8cm/3½in) *S Australia to New Zealand C.* A relatively smooth, rock-dwelling species with fine spiral cords near the sutures and shortened knobs on the shoulders of the whorls. It has brown-and-white-striped varices and the aperture and columella are entirely white.

3 *CYMATIUM PYRUM* **Pear Triton** *L. 1758* (9cm/3½in) *Indo-Pacific C.* This dweller on coral or sand is brick-red or orange and has coarse spiral ridges. There are strong teeth on the inside of the outer lip.

4 *CYMATIUM LOTORIUM* **Black Spotted Triton** *L. 1758* (to 12cm/4¾in) *Indo-Pacific C.* A coarsely knobbed, heavy, and thick shell with particularly prominent knobs on the body whorl. It lives among coral in shallow water.

5 *CYMATIUM BOSCHI* **Bosch's Triton** *Abbott and Lewis 1970* (10cm/4in) *Oman U.* The shell has coarse nodulose spiral ridges, a medium-height spire, and a very long siphonal canal. Its aperture is white and the oval operculum is dark brown. There are flat shoulder ridges to the suture on each whorl.

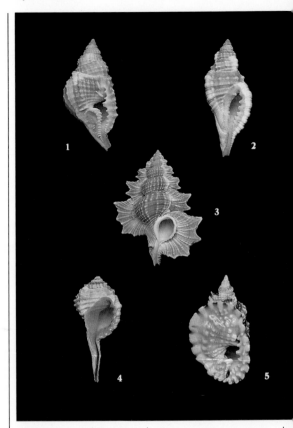

1 *DISTORSIO CLATHRATA* **Atlantic Distorsio** *Lamarck 1816* (6cm/2¼in) *Caribbean to NE Brazil C.* An inhabitant of deep water to over 100m (330ft) with a beige-white coloration and coarse knobs and cords.

2 *CYMATIUM KREBSII* **Krebs's Triton** *Mörch 1877* (6cm/2¼in) *Caribbean U.* This species dwells in offshore and deep water, where it is brought up in fishing nets. It is beige to white, with coarse spiral ridges, and has an extended siphonal canal and a strongly toothed aperture.

3 *BIPLEX PERCA* **Winged Frog** *Perry 1811* (to 7cm/2¾in) *W Pacific C.* Fished from relatively deep water, this is a distinctively shaped species with flattened, ridged, and extended varices

which resemble leaves.

4 *CYMATIUM GUTTURNIUM* **Long-necked Triton** *Röding 1798* (7cm/2¾in) *W Pacific C.* An offshore dweller, this shell is white to beige, with strong spiral cords. It has an extended siphonal canal, a deep-orange aperture, and a callused parietal wall.

5 *DISTORSIO ANUS* **Old Lady Shell** *L. 1758* (to 7cm/2¾in) *Indo-Pacific C.* An attractive species, with a relatively high spire and a wide, enlarged body whorl. The aperture, columella, and parietal wall are callused and extended to form a flattened shield area. It is found in shallow water in corals.

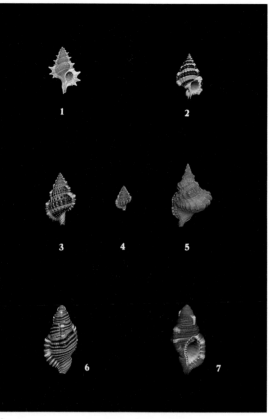

1 *BIPLEX ACULEATUM Schepman 1909* (3cm/1¼in) *Japan to Australia U.* Fished from deep water, this species is smaller and finer than Biplex perca and the varices are shorter and more pointed.

2 *GYRINEUM GYRINUM* **Tadpole Triton** *L. 1758* (2cm/⅜in) *Indo-Pacific C.* Found in shallow water under corals, this shell has broad, vivid brown spiral bands on a cream-yellow background.

3 *GYRINEUM TUBERCULATA* **Knobbed Gyrineum** *Röding 1798* (3cm/1¼in) *Indo-Pacific C.* A shallow-water dweller with pustulated spiral bands on an overall cream-brown background.

4 *GYRINEUM ROSEUM* **Rose Gyrineum** *Reeve 1844* (2cm/⅜in) *Indo-Pacific U.* This small shell, with a delicate pink-orange coloration, lives under corals in shallow water.

5 *DISTORSIO KURZI* **Kurz's Distorsio** *Petuch and Harasewych 1980* (3cm/1¼in) *Philippines U.* A deep-water species only recently described. It is generally orange-brown.

6 *CYMATIUM HEPATICUM* **Black Striped Triton** *Röding 1798* (4.5cm/1¾in) *Indo-Pacific C.* A small, pretty species found on coral reefs. It has spiral beading of dark brown and orange.

7 *CYMATIUM RUBECULA* **Red Triton** *L. 1758* (4cm/1½in) *Indo-Pacific C.* The species is almost identical in shape and sculpturing to *Cymatium hepaticum* but its coloration is an overall bright red with white splashes on the varices and lip margins.

Bursidae The Frog shells, although similar in appearance to the Ranellidae, differ in that they have a canal at the posterior end of the aperture. The anterior canal is short. These carnivores live mainly in shallow water in corals and rocks.

1 *BUFONARIA NOBILIS Reeve 1844* (to 9cm/3½in) *W Pacific C.* This thick, coarsely sculptured species has prominent spiral beads and nodules and raised, sharp varices. It is mottled brown and beige.

2 *BURSA RUBETA* **Red-mouthed Frog** *Röding 1798* (to 12cm/4¾in) *Indo-Pacific C.* A generally solid shell with coarse spiral ridges and knobs and a high spire. The aperture is orange, the columella plicate, and the outer edge of the lip denticulate.

3 *BURSA BUFONIA* **Warted Frog** *Gmelin 1791* (6cm/2½in) *Indo-Pacific C.* A small, heavy shell with solid nodules on the shoulders and a prominent, upturned posterior canal on each varix. It lives under corals.

4 *BURSA RANA* **Common Frog** *L. 1758* (to 10cm/4in) *Indo-Pacific C.* A solid, beige-white shell with fine spiral beading, sharp nodules on the whorl shoulders, and spines on the varices and the outer lip.

5 *BURSA CALIFORNICA* **Californian Frog** *Hinds 1843* (10cm/4in) *California to Mexico U.* An inhabitant of offshore rocks, this species is off-white and has a white aperture. It has sharp nodules on the shoulders, spiral beading and cords, and there is occasionally pale-brown banding.

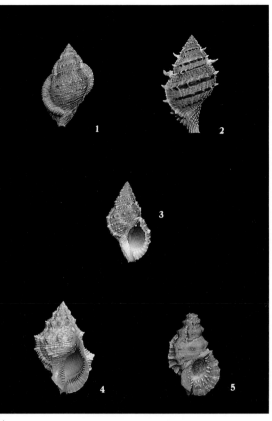

1 *BURSA MARGARITULA* **Noble Frog** *Deshayes 1832* (5cm/2in) *Indo-Pacific* **C**. This thick and solid species lives under corals. It has spiral beading, plicate columella, a denticulate outer lip, and a white aperture.

2 *BURSA ELEGANS* **Elegant Frog** *Sowerby 1835* (7cm/2¾in) *Indian Ocean* **C**. This attractive species lives in shallow water and has spiral beading and cords and sharp spines on the shoulders and varices. The background colour is beige and there are two or three rows of dark-brown bands.

3 *BURSA AWATII* **Bohol Frog** *Ray 1949* (7cm/2¾in) *Central Philippines* **U**. Having a restricted range, this shell has only recently become available in any numbers. It is pale-brown-

beige and very thin and light.

4 *BURSA CRUMENA FOLIATA* **Frilly Frog** *Broderip 1825* (7cm/2¾in) *Indian Ocean* **C**. A coarsely sculptured, fawn-white shell with a vivid orange aperture, distinctly plicate columella and outer lip, and a half-moon-shaped operculum.

5 *BURSA CORRUGATA* **Corrugated Frog** *Perry 1811* (5cm/2in) *Caribbean to Brazil; W Africa* **U**. A solid, thick, orange-brown shell which is in many cases truncated. The flaring lip and callused parietal area are covered with white plicae and denticles. It is found on rocks to a depth of 25m (80ft).

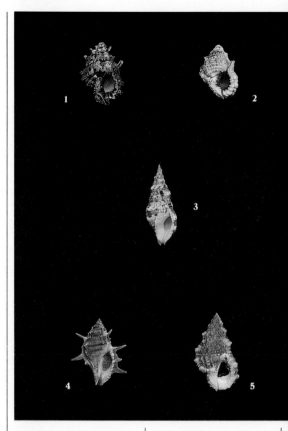

1 *Bursa lamarcki* **Lamarck's Frog** *Deshayes 1853* (5cm/2in) *SW Pacific C.* This thick and coarsely sculptured species has extended, upturned posterior canals. It is a mottled black-brown and has a very dark plicate and denticulate aperture.

2 *Bursa mammata* **Mammal Frog** *Röding 1798* (6cm/2¼in) *W Pacific C.* A small, solid, off-white shell which inhabits reefs, this species is coarsely sculptured and has a distinctive purple aperture with cream surrounds.

3 *Colubraria muricata* **Maculated False Triton** *Lightfoot 1786* (7cm/2¾in) *Indian Ocean U.* A tall, slender shell with spiral beading and cords. There are brown and beige blotches, the aperture is cream, and the inner

lip is denticulate.

4 *Bursa echinata* **Spiny Frog** *Link 1807* (5cm/2in) *Indian Ocean C.* A dull-brown offshore dweller with sharp shoulder nodules, extended spines on the outer lip and varices, and a white aperture.

5 *Bursa granularis* **Granulate Frog** *Röding 1798* (to 7cm/2¾in) *Indo-Pacific and Caribbean C.* The coloration is a mottled orange-brown with a white aperture. The shell has spiral beading and short nodules and the spire is tall.

Muricidae This is a very large
family, with numerous genera, in
which size and shape vary greatly
from very spinose shells to plain
species with little or no
sculpturing. They dwell mainly in
shallow water, among rocks and
corals, and all are carnivorous,
preying on molluscs by boring a
hole through the shell and
devouring the contents.
Classification of this group has
long proved problematic.
1 *MUREX SCOLOPAX* **Woodcock
Murex** *Dillwyn 1817* (12cm/4¾in)
Red Sea C. A pale-beige-white
shell with short, slightly upturned
spines on the spire and body
whorl. There are longer spines on
the long canal. The species' range
is restricted.
2 *MUREX ADUNCOSPINOSUS*

Short-spined Murex *Sowerby
1841* (8cm/3¼in) *W Pacific C.* A
shorter species than Murex
tribulus, with stunted spines and
coarse spiral cording. It is an
overall brown-grey and has a
white aperture.
3 *MUREX PECTEN* **Venus Comb**
Lightfoot 1786 (to 15cm/6in) *Indo-
Pacific C.* A collectors' favourite,
this shell has a moderately high
spire, a long, straight siphonal
canal, and spiral cording. There
are three varices per whorl, each
bearing many long, sharp spines.
4 *MUREX TROSCHELI* **Troschel's
Murex** *Lischke 1868* (to
15cm/6in) *W Pacific C.* This
striking shell is similar to *Murex
pecten*, but has fewer spines.
There is spiral cording, with
brown bands.

1 *MUREX TWEEDIANUS* **Tweed Murex** Macpherson 1962 (to 7cm/2¾in) *E Australia C.* A pretty pink shell which is coarsely sculptured, but generally light, and has raised, spiral, white noduled bands. The siphonal canal is short.

2 *MUREX HIRASEI* **Hirase's Murex** Hirase 1915 (6cm/2¼in) *Japan to Taiwan U.* An offshore species, sturdy and with strong spiral cording. The canal is elongate, recurved, and slender.

3 *MUREX NIGROSPINUS* **Black-spined Murex** Reeve 1845 *SW Pacific C.* A shallow-water species with a moderately tall spire, spiral ridges on the whorls, and about three axial ribs between the varices. There are blackened tips to the longer varix spines.

4 *MUREX HAUSTELLUM* **Snipe's Bill** L. 1758 (12cm/4¾in) *Indo-Pacific C.* A shallow-water species with a depressed spire, a bulbous body whorl, and a very long canal. It has spiral cording, axial ribs, and brown lines and blotches. The aperture is pink.

5 *MUREX CABRITII* **Cabrit's Murex** Bernardi 1859 (5cm/2in) *Florida to Caribbean C.* This offshore dweller is dainty and pinkish, with spiral ridges and low axial ribs. There are a few short spines on the spire and body whorl and longer spines in three rows on the canal.

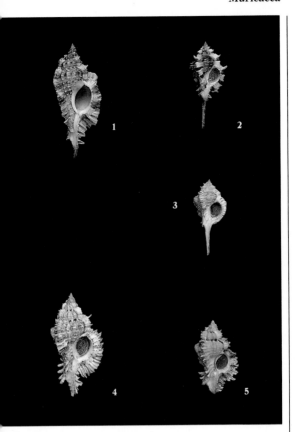

1 *NAQUETIA BARCLAYI* **Barclay's Murex** *Reeve 1858* (8cm/3¼in) *Philippines* **U**. A one-time rarity, with a restricted range, this shell is thin and light and has a high spire. The canal is extended and there are flattened, frilled varices at right angles to the whorls. The outer lip is frilled to the lower end of the canal.

2 *SIRATUS MOTACILLA* **Wagtail Murex** *Gmelin 1791* (6cm/2¼in) *Caribbean* **U**. A particularly attractive species which is caught in traps in deep water and which, when fresh, is red, orange and cream. It has short, sharp spines on the varices, fine spiral cords and strong axial ribs, and a long, thin canal.

3 *SIRATUS PERELEGANS* *E. Vokes 1965* (6cm/2¼in) *Caribbean* **U**. This shell inhabits relatively deep water and is similar in shape to *Siratus motacilla*, but is off-white with distinct, fine brown spiral lines. It has strong axial ribs.

4 *CHICOMUREX SUPERBUS* **Superb Murex** *Sowerby 1889* (6cm/2¼in) *Taiwan to Philippines* **U**. This offshore dweller has coarse ornamentation of raised spiral cords, axial ridges, and denticulate, occasionally frilled, varices.

5 *SIRATUS LACINIATUS* **Fringed Murex** *Sowerby 1841* (to 6cm/2¼in) *Indo-Pacific* **U**. A thick, coarsely sculptured shell with spiral ridges and axial ribs, this species is found in shallow water. It has frilled varices and a purple aperture and is often heavily encrusted.

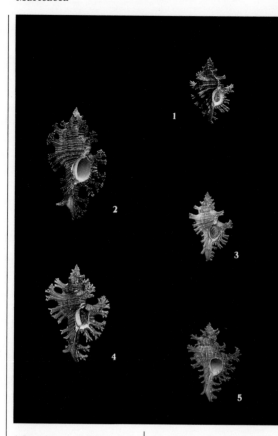

1 *CHICOREUS MAURUS Broderip
1833* (7cm/2⅞in) *Central Pacific* **U**.
A short, thick, very angular shell
which is basically brown with
pink-tipped varices. It has a fairly
restricted range.
2 *CHICOREUS PALMAROSAE* **Rose
Branched Murex** *Lamarck 1822*
(10cm/4in) *Philippines* **C**. The
Philippine variety of this species
is quite different from the Sri
Lankan. It is an overall brown,
sometimes dark, is less frondose,
and there is a complete absence of
pink in its coloration.
3 *CHICOREUS SAULII* **Saul's
Murex** *Sowerby 1841* (to
10cm/4in) *SW Pacific* **U**. This
offshore species is solid, slightly
elongate, and has spiral cording.
It is generally light brown with a
pinkish tinge and the varices are

frondose and pink.
4 *CHICOREUS PALMAROSAE* **Rose
Branched Murex** *Lamarck 1822*
(10cm/4in) *Sri Lanka* **U**. One of
the most beautiful of all shells,
although very difficult to clean,
this species has coarse sculpturing
and thick spines on varices which
are prettily frondose and deep
pink in colour.
5 *CHICOREUS SPECTRUM Reeve
1846* (10cm/4in) *E South America*
R. This brown-beige shell is
similar in appearance to *Chicoreus
palma rosae*, but is generally less
frondose and has longer spines on
the varices.

1 *HEXAPLEX NIGRITUS* **Black Murex** *Philippi 1845* (to 15cm/6in) *California to Mexico* **C**. A thick and heavy shell, distinctively marked with vivid black and white spiral stripes and bands. The axial spines are coarse and blunt, with black tips.

2 *HEXAPLEX RADIX* **Radish Murex** *Gmelin 1791* (to 12cm/4¾in) *W Central America* **C**. Some experts suggest that this shallow-water dweller is a more southerly form of *Hexaplex nigritus*. It is generally smaller, more rounded, and has more, sharper, black spines.

3 *HEXAPLEX ERYTHROSTOMUS* **Pink-mouthed Murex** *Swainson 1831* (to 11cm/4¼in) *California to Mexico* **C**. Generally found in shallow water, this shell also occurs in deep water, in which case it has longer spines. It is a popular shell, globose and off-white with a deep-pink aperture and parietal area.

4 *HEXAPLEX DUPLEX* *Röding 1798* (to 13cm/5in) *W Africa* **U**. A large and rather sturdy shell, this species is usually beige-brown with a pink aperture, although occasionally it is an overall orange-red with a deep-red aperture. It is an offshore dweller.

5 *HEXAPLEX REGIUS* **Royal Murex** *Swainson 1821* (to 16cm/6¼in) *W Central America* **C**. A handsome, solid, heavy, and globose shell which is an overall off-white with a vivid pink aperture. The heavily callused columella is pink and the upper area is chocolate brown.

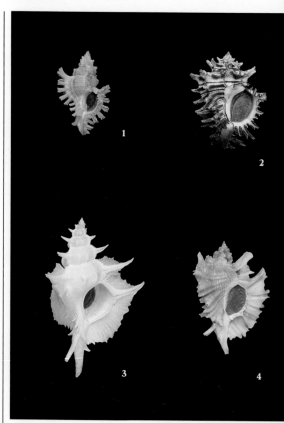

1 *CHICOREUS RUBIGINOSUS* **Red Murex** *Reeve 1845* (8cm/3¼in) *SW Pacific* **U**. This dweller in relatively shallow water occurs in a wide variety of colours, from pure white, through pink and cream, to deep orange. It has a fairly high spire and fine spiral cords. There are three varices on each whorl and they have frondose spines, particularly on the body whorl.

2 *HEXAPLEX PRINCEPS* **Prince Murex** *Broderip 1833* (10cm/4in) *W Central America* **U**. An attractive thick shell with a moderately high spire and a relatively long siphonal canal. There are between five and seven varices to each whorl. The varices are spinose and some are long, particularly at the shoulders.

3 *SIRATUS ALABASTER* **Alabaster Murex** *Reeve 1845* (13cm/5in) *Taiwan to Philippines* **U**. A beautiful species and a favourite with collectors, this shell was at one time a great rarity but has become more readily available within the last 20 years. It is usually fished from deep water in tangle nets and the very fine wing-like varices often remain surprisingly intact during the process.

4 *CERATOSTOMA BURNETTI* **Burnett's Murex** *Adams and Reeve 1849* (to 10cm/4in) *Japan to Korea* **U**. This striking shell is rather angular and thick, with spiral ridges extending on to spectacular wing-like extensions on each varix, of which there are three to each whorl.

1 *HOMALOCANTHA ZAMBOI*
Zambo's Murex *Burch and
Burch 1960* (5cm/2in) *Philippines
C*. A shallow-water species, off-
white with a pink aperture. The
spire is short, the canal is long,
and there are about five varices to
each whorl, bearing long, hollow
projections which are flattened at
their tips.

2 *CHICOREUS CICHOREUM* **Endive
Murex** *Gmelin 1791* (10cm/4in)
SW Pacific C. This species ranges
in colour from pure white to a
vivid brown-and-white-banded
form. The ornamentation of the
varices is also variable, some
having few spines, others many.

3 *PTERYNOTUS ELONGATUS*
Clavus Murex *Lightfoot 1786*
(8cm/3¼in) *SW Pacific C*. A choice
collectors' item, this reef-dwelling

shell has an unusual form, being
generally very elongated with a
tall, slender spire and an extended
canal. The body-whorl varices are
flaring and finely ribbed.

4 *CHICOREUS ASIANUS* **Asian
Murex** *Kuroda 1942* (to
10cm/4in) *Japan to Taiwan C*. An
off-white to brown offshore
dweller with fine spiral cords and
three varices to each whorl. The
varices bear long and short frilled
spines. The siphonal canal is long.

5 *CHICOREUS CNISSODUS* *Euthyme
1889* (7cm/2¾in) *W Pacific U*. A
delicately ornamented coral-reef
dweller with axial ribs and strong
spiral cords with fine brown
bands. The varices have sharp,
sometimes recurved, spines. The
spire is tall and the siphonal canal
is extended.

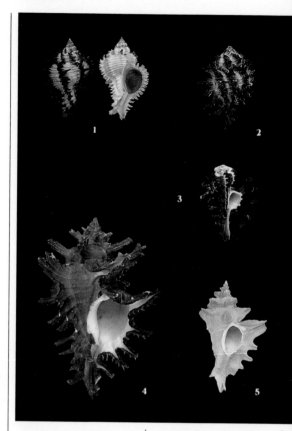

1 *CHICOREUS STAINFORTHI*
Stainforth's Murex *Reeve 1843*
(6cm/2¼in) *N and W Australia C.*
Occasionally white or pinkish, the
ground colour of this shallow-
water shell is more often cream.
The shell has spiral ribs and there
are six or seven varices bearing
many short, sharp, recurved
black spines on each whorl.

2 *HOMALOCANTHA*
MELANAMATHOS Gmelin 1791 (to
5cm/2in) *W Africa R.* This
offshore dweller is pear-shaped,
with a low spire and an extended
canal. There are eight or more
varices bearing short, dark-
brown-black spines on each
whorl.

3 *HOMALOCANTHA SCORPIO*
Scorpion Murex *L. 1758* (4cm/
1½in) *SW Pacific C.* Usually dark

brown but occasionally white,
this small shell inhabits shallow
water. It has a depressed spire, an
extended canal, and between five
and seven varices on each whorl,
the last three bearing long,
flattened spines.

4 *CHICOREUS MEGACERUS*
Megacerus Murex *Sowerby
1834* (to 9cm/3½in) *W Africa U.* A
coarse, brown shell with a white
aperture and about four varices,
bearing sharp, hollow spines, on
each whorl. The species lives in
shallow water.

5 *PTEROPURPURA CENTRIFUGA*
Centrifuge Murex *Hinds 1844*
(6cm/2¼in) *California to Mexico U.*
An off-white shell with very fine
spiral cords. It is found offshore to
a depth of 25m (80ft). Each varix
bears flat, blade-like projections.

1 *CHICOREUS AXICORNIS Lamarck 1822* (to 7cm/2¾in) *Japan to Philippines* **C**. This offshore species has a high spire and an elongated canal. There are three varices on each whorl with short and long frondose and recurved spines.

2 *CHICOREUS CORRUGATUS Sowerby 1841* (5cm/2in) *Red Sea* **R**. This shell has coarse spiral ribs. There are three varices, each bearing sharp, slightly upturned spines, on each whorl.

3 *HOMALOCANTHA OXYACANTHA Broderip 1833* (5cm/2in) *W Central America* **U**. A beige-white shallow-water species, usually pear-shaped. It has a depressed spire, a relatively long, almost closed canal, and five or six varices on each whorl, each bearing up to 12 spines of varying length.

4 *PTERYNOTUS MIYOKOAE* **Miyoko Murex** *Kosuge 1979* (to 6cm/2¼in) *Central Philippines* **R**. A much sought-after collectors' item, this shell was at one time almost unobtainable but is now fished occasionally in deep water.

5 *CHICOREUS CERVICORNIS* **Stag Horn Murex** *Lamarck 1822* (to 6cm/2¼in) *N and W Australia* **U**. A collectors' favourite, this species has a moderate spire, a long canal, and three varices with spines on each whorl.

6 *HEXAPLEX TRUNCULUS* **Dye Murex** *L. 1758* (7cm/2¾in) *Mediterranean* **C**. One of the two species used to produce Tyrian purple dye, this thick, coarse shell inhabits shallow water.

93

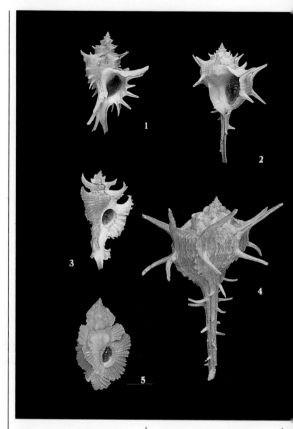

1 *POIRIERIA ZELANDICUS* **New Zealand Murex** *Quoy and Gaimard 1833* (5cm/2in) *New Zealand* **U**. A very thin, light, and spinose offshore dweller. Highly spinose examples are much prized by collectors.

2 *BOLINUS BRANDARIS* **Dye Murex** *L. 1758* (8cm/3¼in) *Mediterranean* **A**. In ancient times the fluid from this shell was extracted for use in the production of Tyrian purple dye. Some examples are spinose, others spineless.

3 *PURPURELLUS GAMBIENSIS* **Gambia Murex** *Reeve 1845* (to 7cm/2¾in) *W Africa* **U**. This shell has an interesting shape. The spire is of medium height and the canal is elongated. There are three varices, each of which bears upturned, sometimes flattened, spines, while the body-whorl varices also bear wing-like, fluted projections.

4 *BOLINUS CORNUTUS* **Horned Murex** *L. 1758* (to 15cm/6in) *W Africa* **U**. Not dissimilar to *Bolinus brandaris*, although much larger and heavier, this offshore species has a depressed spire, a large body whorl, and a very long canal. It has long, sometimes recurved, spines.

5 *PTERYNOTUS LOEBBECKEI* **Loebbecke's Murex** *Kobelt 1879* (5cm/2in) *China Sea to Philippines* **R**. Until recent years this deep-water species was a great rarity and is still much sought after. It has beautiful flaring, winged varices, fine spiral lirae, and axial ribs.

1 *CHICOREUS ORCHIDIFLORUS*
Orchid Murex *Shikama 1973*
(3cm/1¼in) *Philippines* **R**. This
deep-water shell is small, thin,
and very light. It is pale orange
and has long, fine, lirate varices
which are almost transparent.
2 *HEXAPLEX ANGULARIS* **Angled
Murex** *Lamarck 1822* (4cm/1½in)
W Africa **U**. A shallow-water
species with small and rather
sturdy spiral ribs. Each whorl has
about six short-spined varices.
The shell is orange or brown.
3 *PTERYNOTUS PELLUCIDUS Reeve
1845* (5cm/2in) *Indo-Pacific* **U**. A
thin, off-white shell which lives in
relatively shallow water. It has a
very small aperture and flaring,
fan-like varices on the last two
whorls.
4 *CHICOREUS NOBILIS Shikama*

1977 (to 5cm/2in) *Japan to
Philippines* **C**. A small, delicately
fronded species found in offshore
waters.
5 *CHICOREUS ROSSITERI*
Rossiter's Murex *Crosse 1872*
(to 5cm/2in) *Japan to Philippines*
U. Originally confused with
Chicoreus nobilis, this shallow-
water dweller is more elongate,
with a high spire and a very long
canal. Each of the three varices
bears finger-like projections or
spines.
6 *CHICOMUREX VENUSTULUS
Rehder and Wilson 1975* (5cm/2in)
Philippines **U**. This delicate and
beautiful collectors' item has a
high spire and a long, recurved
canal. The coloration varies from
beige to deep pink, and some
examples are banded.

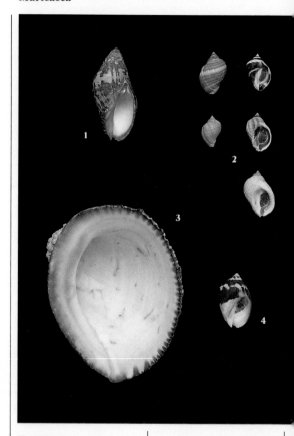

Thaididae These shells are solid and small-to-medium in size, have low spires and large apertures, and lack varices. They live among rocks and corals in shallow water and are all carnivorous, eating other seashells.

1 *NASSA FRANCOLINA* **Francolina Jopas** *Bruguière 1789* (to 6cm/2¼in) *Indian Ocean C.* The species has a medium-height spire and a large, ovate body whorl. It is reddish brown with two or more broad spiral areas of beige-pink, and the aperture is white. Most shells are thick and smooth, with fine spiral lirae and many axial growth lines.

2 *NUCELLA LAPILLUS* **Atlantic Dog Whelk** *L. 1758* (4cm/1½in) *NW and NE Atlantic A.* The coloration of this shell varies from white to yellow or brown, and, some examples have broad bands. The species lives on intertidal rocks, often among colonies of mussels, on which it feeds.

3 *CONCHOLEPAS CONCHOLEPAS* **Barnacle Rock Shell** *Bruguière 1792* (10cm/4in) *W South America C.* A shore dweller, this species is similar to the limpets and abalones – it attaches itself to rocks by its strong foot.

4 *THAIS MELONES* **Gourd Rock Shell** *Duclos 1832* (5cm/2in) *W Central America C.* An inhabitant of rocks in the intertidal zone, this shell has a low spire, a large, rounded body whorl, and fine spiral cords. The coloration is cream with very wide, sometimes unbroken, spiral bands of black.

1 *THAIS TUBEROSA* **Knobbed Rock Shell** *Röding 1798* (5cm/2in) *W and Central Pacific* **C**. This species lives among corals and is generally creamy white with brown axial stripes. The spire is low and there are spiral ridges and strong, blunt spines on the shoulder.

2 *RAPANA BEZOAR L. 1758* (7cm/2¾in) *Japan and China Sea* **C**. An offshore dweller with a beige coloration and coarse spiral ridges both outside and within. The spire is short, the body whorl and aperture are enlarged, and the umbilicus is deep.

3 *PURPURA PLANOSPIRA* **Judas Eye** *Lamarck 1822* (to 6cm/2¼in) *W Central America and Galapagos Islands* **R**. Seldom seen in amateur collections, this spectacular shell virtually lacks a spire and has an enlarged body whorl and a flaring aperture.

4 *NEORAPANA MURICATA* **Frilled purpura** *Broderip 1832* (6cm/2¼in) *W Central America* **C**. This dweller in intertidal waters has a depressed spire and an angled shoulder, smooth spiral cording with five or six blunt, knobbed ridges, and axial lamellations.

5 *PURPURA PATULA* **Wide-mouthed Purpura** *L. 1758* (to 8cm/3¼in) *Caribbean* **C**. The interior of this inhabitant of intertidal rocks is white-grey, while the columella and parietal wall are pale orange. There are coarse spiral ridges, some with low nodules, and the lip is dentate. The spire is low, with a large body whorl and aperture.

97

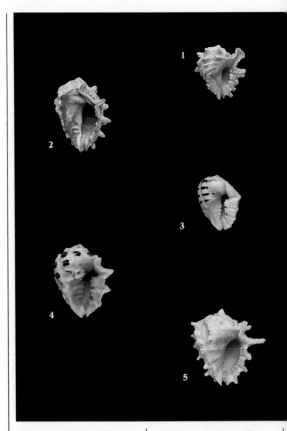

1 *DRUPA GROSSULARIA* **Finger Drupe** *Röding 1798* (2.5cm/1in) *SW Pacific* **C**. A shallow-reef dweller with an orange interior. There are coarse spiral ridges, the lip is dentate with exterior frondose projections, and the anal canal is extended.

2 *DRUPA CLATHRATA* **Clathrate Drupe** *Lamarck 1816* (4cm/1½in) *SW Pacific* **U**. An intertidal species with an encrusted, nodulose exterior and a lavender interior. The coloration around the inner lip edge and the parietal wall is white and light brown. The lip is dentate and there are columellar plaits.

3 *DROPA MORUM IODOSTOMA Lesson 1840* (3.5cm/1⅜in) *Central Pacific* **U**. A globose shell, spirally corded, and beige, with about five broad black spiral bands. The interior and columella are pale lavender. The aperture is narrow and the inner lip is denticulate.

4 *DRUPA MORUM* **Purple Drupe** *Röding 1798* (4cm/1½in) *Indo-Pacific* **C**. Often heavily encrusted, this shell has a coarse, nodulose, black-and-white exterior and a narrow, vivid purple aperture with thickened denticles. It is found on coral reefs.

5 *DRUPA RUBUSIDAEUS* **Rose Drupe** *Röding 1798* (4cm/1½in) *Indo-Pacific* **C**. The exterior is chalky-white, the interior bright pink, and the dentate inner lip cream. There are coarse spiral ridges bearing rows of short, sharp spines. The species inhabits intertidal reefs.

Coralliophilidae This group, popular with collectors, includes many beautifully sculptured and ornamented shells which inhabit both shallow and very deep water – sometimes to depths greater than 300m (985ft).

1 *LATIAXIS PILSBRYI* **Pilsbry's Latiaxis** *Hirase 1908* (to 4cm/ 1½in) *Japan to Philippines* **R**. This species, popular with collectors, is somewhat similar to *Latiaxis mawae*, but is much smaller and more delicate. It inhabits offshore to deep water.

2 *BABELOMUREX FINCHI* **Finch's Latiaxis** *Fulton 1930* (5cm/2in) *Japan to Taiwan* **C**. This umbilicate deep-water species has spirally ridged, angled shoulders with triangular spines, a white, ridged aperture to the lip edge,

and an open, recurved canal.

3 *RAPA RAPA* **Bubble Turnip** *L. 1758* (7cm/2¾in) *SW Pacific* **C**. A light, fragile, yellow-beige shell which lives inside soft coral. There are coarse spiral ridges and the spire is flat or sunken and the canal long and often recurved.

4 *LATIAXIS MAWAE* **Mawe's Latiaxis** *Gray in Griffith and Pidgeon 1834* (6cm/2¼in) *Japan to Taiwan* **C**. An inhabitant of offshore to deep water, this shell has a flattened spire and an angled spiral shoulder bearing frilled, sometimes recurved, blunt, triangular spines. There is a wide, gaping umbilicus and a long, curved canal. The aperture is smooth white and the exterior has fine spiral lirae.

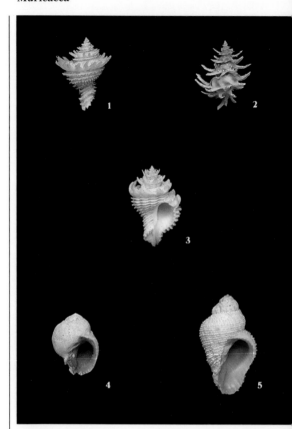

1 *BABELOMUREX LISCHKEANUS*
Lischke's Latiaxis *Dunker 1882*
(to 4cm/1½in) *Japan to New
Zealand; South Africa* **U**. A
beautifully ornamented shell with
spinose spiral cords and curved,
triangular shoulder spines, this is
a favourite with collectors. It lives
in deep water.

2 *LATIAXIS SPINOSUS* **Pagoda
Latiaxis** *Hirase 1908* (3cm/1⅛in)
Japan to Philippines **C**. A very
fine, light shell, with a high spire
and an elongated canal. The
angled shoulders bear long,
recurved spines. The umbilicate
fasciole also bears long spines. The
species inhabits deep water.

3 *BABELOMUREX JAPONICUS*
Japanese Latiaxis *Dunker 1882*
(to 4cm/1½in) *Japan to Taiwan* **U**.
Similar to *Latiaxis lischkeanus*

but thicker and with a greater
amount of coarse spiral ribbing,
this species is found in both
shallow and deeper water to 200m
(655ft). The shoulder spines are
either blunt or long and recurved.

4 *CORALLIOPHILA VIOLACEA*
Purple Coral Snail *Kiener 1836*
(3cm/1⅛in) *Indo-Pacific* **C**. A
squat, globose shell, usually
heavily encrusted. It has a flaring,
vivid purple aperture and is found
on coral reefs.

5 *CORALLIOPHILA RADULA* **Pear-
shaped Coral Snail** *A. Adams
1855* (to 5cm/2in) *Japan to
Philippines* **U**. An offshore to
deep-water dweller with a
moderate spire and an open, flat
canal. The fine, spinose spiral
cords are often encrusted. The
aperture is a beautiful purple.

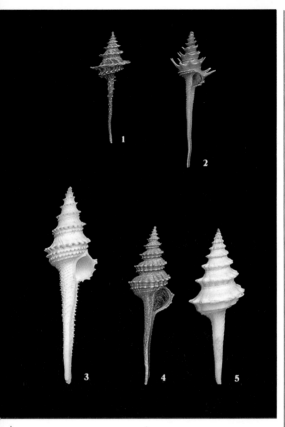

Columbariidae A small family of mostly rare deep-water shells with high spires and very long siphonal canals.

1 *COLUMBARIUM SPINICINCTUM* **Spined Pagoda Shell** *von Martens 1881* (6cm/2¼in) *Australia* **U**. This species is fine and light, with a high, slim spire and body whorl, and the canal is long and thin. The whorls and the shoulder are spinose. There are brown axial markings on a cream background.

2 *COLUMBARIUM PAGODA* **Pagoda Shell** *Lesson 1831* (6cm/2¼in) *Japan to Taiwan* **C**. An offshore dweller with a high spire and a very long and delicate canal. The angled whorls and shoulder are sharply spinose.

3 *COLUMBARIUM HARRISAE* **Harris's Pagoda Shell**

Harasewych 1983 (to 10cm/4in) *Australia* **R**. Probably the largest species in the genus, this shell has convex whorls, spiral ribs which are beaded and spinose, and a very long, finely spinose canal. It inhabits deep water.

4 *COLUMBARIUM SPIRALIS* **Spiral Pagoda Shell** *A. Adams 1856* (8cm/3¼in) *New Zealand* **R**. A very light, delicate species with rounded, finely spinose whorls, a high spire, and a long, thin canal. It lives in offshore to deep water.

5 *COLUMBARIUM EASTWOODAE* **Eastwood's Pagoda Shell** *Kilburn 1971* (5cm/2in) *South Africa* **C**. A chalky-white shell which inhabits deep water, this species has a high spire and a long canal. The sharply angled whorls bear blunt, flat crenulations.

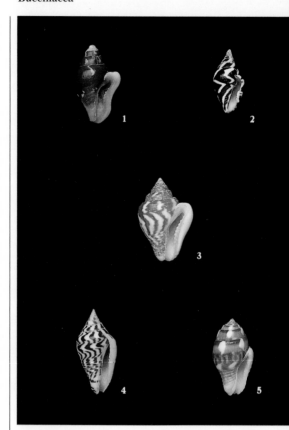

Columbellidae Sometimes referred to as Pyrenidae, the Dove Shells are fairly small and colourful snails which inhabit tropical and sub-tropical seas. There are many species, generally carnivorous, and their habitat is sand or coral.

1 *COLUMBELLA HAEMASTOMA* **Blood-stained Dove Shell** *Sowerby 1832* (2cm/⅘in) *W Central America* **U**. An intertidal species which lives under rocks, this shell is solid and thick, with a high spire. It is rich brown with a white, concave lip and the aperture and columella are stained orange.

2 *PYRENE OCELLATA* **Lightning Dove Shell** *Link 1807* (2cm/⅘in) *Indo-Pacific* **C**. A shallow-water dweller with a high spire, a tapering body whorl, and minute denticles on the interior of the lip.

3 *COLUMBELLA STROMBIFORMIS* **Stromboid Dove Shell** *Lamarck 1822* (2.5cm/1in) *W Central America* **C**. This shell is similar to *Columbella haemastoma* but is brown with white axial zigzag lines on the body whorl.

4 *PYRENE PHILIPPINARUM* **Philippine Dove Shell** *Reeve 1843* (2.5cm/1in) *SW Pacific* **U**. An intertidal species, white with dark-brown and wavy axial stripes, a high-pointed spire, and a rather long, tapering body.

5 *PYRENE FLAVA* **Yellow Dove Shell** *Bruguière 1789* (2.5cm/1in) *Indo-Pacific* **C**. This solid, smooth shallow-water shell has a few spiral ridges on the anterior part of the body whorl.

Buccinidae The Whelks are a large and varied family represented in both warm and cold seas. Some are drab, while others are highly colourful. All are carnivorous, feeding on molluscs and echinoderms.

1 *PLICIFUSUS PLICATUS* **Plicate Colus** *A. Adams 1863* (5cm/2in) *Japan C.* A dweller in cold-water areas to a depth of 100m (330ft), this shell is a pale-grey-brown with fine spiral lirae and slightly curved axial ribs. The spire is tall and the siphonal canal short.

2 *BUCCINUM UNDATUM* **Edible European Whelk** *L. 1758* (to 10cm/4in) *NW and NE Atlantic A.* Fished commercially for food, this species inhabits shallow to deep water. The spire is slightly variable but is generally high.

There are spiral ridges with fine axial ribs on the early whorls.

3 *PHOS SENTICOSUS* **Phos Whelk** *L. 1758* (4cm/1½in) *Indo-Pacific C.* Similar to *Phos crassus*, but more delicate, with coarse spiral cords and lamellate axial ribs. It lives in sand or mud.

4 *BUCCINUM GRAMMATUS* **Grammatus Whelk** *Dall 1907* (10cm/4in) *Japan R.* A cold-water species usually covered with a dark-brown, flaky periostracum. The shell is white underneath. It has coarse, deeply grooved spiral ribs.

5 *PHOS CRASSUS* *Hinds 1843* (5cm/2in) *W Central America C.* This robust shell is fawn to dark brown and has a high spire. It has spiral cords and strong axial ribs which are nodules on the body whorl.

1 *NEPTUNEA ANTIQUA* **Ancient Neptune** *L. 1758 NE Atlantic and North Sea* **C**. A thick, fusiform shell with a tall spire and a wide, flaring aperture. It has fine spiral, and sometimes axial, striae, is a drab grey-white, and is often encrusted. It lives in shallow to deep water.

2 *CANTHARUS MELANOSTOMUS* **Black-mouthed Goblet** *Sowerby 1825* (5cm/2in) *Indian Ocean* **C**. A coarsely sculptured shell with strong spiral ridges and axial ribs and a moderate spire. The columella are stained dark-brown-black.

3 *CANTHARUS TRANQUEBARICUS* **Tranquebar Goblet Whelk** *Gmelin 1791* (4cm/1½in) *Indian Ocean* **C**. This robust shell has a short spire and there are pronounced axial ribs and spiral cording. An inhabitant of shallow water, it is white to yellowish, with a fine orange surround to the white aperture.

4 *NEPTUNEA KUROSHIO Oyama 1958* (8cm/3¼in) *Japan* **C**. A heavy, bulbous, white shell with a short spire, a large aperture, raised spiral ridges, and a short, recurved siphonal canal.

5 *NEPTUNEA TABULATA* **Tabled Neptune** *Baird 1863* (8cm/3¼in) *W North America* **U**. A species which inhabits relatively deep water, this shell is an overall white or beige and has a high spire and a wide, recurved siphonal canal. The whorls are rounded and flat-topped with a raised spiral ridge. There are fine spiral lirae.

1 *BABYLONIA AMBULACRUM*
Walkway Babylon *Sowerby
1825* (4cm/1½in) *W Pacific* **U**. The
shell is similar to *Babylonia
spirata* but much smaller and
more ovate, with deep sutures. It
is an offshore dweller.
2 *BABYLONIA ZEYLANICA* **Indian
Babylon** *Bruguière 1789* (to 7cm/
2¾in) *Indian Ocean* **C**. This
offshore dweller is generally ovate
and has a tall spire and rounded
whorls. It is white with stark
brown streaks, spots, and wavy
axial lines.
3 *BABYLONIA AREOLATA* **Areola
Babylon** *Link 1807* (7cm/2¾in) *W
Pacific* **C**. A similar shell to
Babylonia spirata but with
shoulders that are less angled and
with deep sutures. The umbilicus
of this shallow-water species is

deep and the coloration is an
overall white with large brown
blotches.
4 *BABYLONIA PAPILLARIS*
Spotted Babylon *Sowerby 1825*
(4cm/1½in) *South Africa* **U**. An
inhabitant of relatively shallow
water, this small, delicate shell
has a high spire and rounded
whorls and is beige-white with
fine spots and blotches.
5 *BABYLONIA SPIRATA*
Channelled Babylon *L. 1758*
(6cm/2¼in) *Indian Ocean* **C**. A
dweller in mud in shallow water,
this species is solid and heavy and
has a short spire. The body whorl
is large and the shoulders are
sharply angled with deep sutures.
The shell is white with orange-
brown blotches, spots, and
streaks.

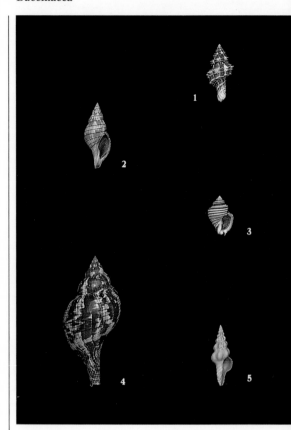

Fasciolariidae Tulip shells are mainly medium to large species, carnivorous, and distributed worldwide, but mainly in tropical waters.

1 *LATIRUS POLYGONUS* **Polygon Latirus** *Gmelin 1791* (7cm/2¾in) *Indo-Pacific C.* An intertidal species with a moderate spire and a long canal. There are spiral ridges with axial ribs, the latter sharp on the shoulders. The shell is white with axial, broken, brown stripes on the ribs.

2 *FASCIOLARIA LILIUM HUNTERIA* **Banded Tulip** *Perry 1811* (8cm/3¼in) *Florida C.* A shallow-water species, smooth and inflated, with a tall spire and a short canal. It has distinct spiral lines with faint blotches of grey-green or peach.

3 *OPEATOSTOMA PSEUDODON*

Thorned Latirus *Burrow 1815* (4cm/1½in) *W Central America C.* A small, robust shell with angular, flattened shoulders and strong spiral ridges of black-brown on white. There is a large tooth at the anterior end of the aperture. The shell is found in rocks at low tide.

4 *FASCIOLARIA TULIPA* **True Tulip** *L. 1758* (15cm/6in) *Caribbean C.* A dweller in sand in shallow water, this large and smooth shell has a tall spire and a long, curved canal.

5 *LATIRUS NODATUS* **Knobbed Latirus** *Gmelin 1791* (7cm/2¾in) *Indo-Pacific C.* This inhabitant of coral reefs is deep pink with a lavender aperture. It is thick, with a tall spire, and has pronounced axial knobs.

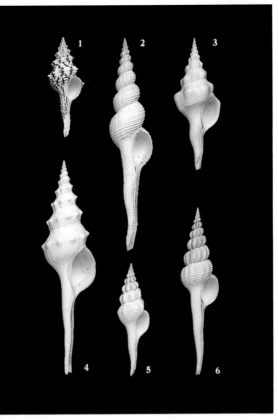

1 *FUSINUS NICOBARICUS* **Nicobar Spindle** *Röding 1798* (12cm/4¾in) *Indo-Pacific* **C**. A short, stocky shell, white with brown, wavy lines. It is found on sand in shallow water and has strong spiral ridges and angled shoulders, the latter sometimes nodulose.

2 *FUSINUS CAPARTI* **Capart's Spindle** *Adam and Knudsen 1969* (to 28cm/11in) *W Africa* **U**. One of the largest shells in the genus, elongated and fusiform. There are rounded whorls, spiral cording, and axial ribs.

3 *FUSINUS UNDATUS* **Wavy Spindle** *Gmelin 1791* (17cm/6⅗in) *SW Pacific* **U**. An offshore dweller with a tall spire and a long canal. There are heavy knobs on the shoulders.

4 *FUSINUS LONGISSIMUS* **Long Spindle** *Gmelin 1791* (28cm/11in) *SW Pacific* **U**. The tall spire and extended canal are characteristic of most of the *Fusinus* species. This is a large shell with angled, nodulose shoulders and spiral cords.

5 *FUSINUS DOWIANUS Olsson 1954* (to 15cm/6in) *Caribbean* **U**. A short, stocky shell, overall white with yellow tints on the first four or five whorls of the spire. There is strong spiral cording with rounded axial ribs.

6 *FUSINUS CRASSIPLICATA* **Ribbed Spindle** *Kira* (to 22cm/9in) *Japan–Taiwan* **U**. This large shell was at one time commonly trawled by Taiwanese fishermen but now seems to be less easy to obtain.

Melongenidae These
carnivorous snails are generally
thick-shelled and medium to
large. They are mainly found in
shallow muddy or brackish water,
often near mangroves, where they
feed on other shells, such as
oysters and clams.

1 *SYRINX ARUANUS* **Australian
Trumpet** *L. 1758* (to 60cm/24in)
N Australia **C.** This, the largest
gastropod shell in the world,
inhabits a restricted area between
northern Australia and southern
New Guinea with its centre in the
Torres Straits. The habitat varies
from intertidal zones to depths of
more than 50m (165ft) and the
shell is often taken by prawn
fishermen. In recent years
Taiwanese trawlers have
"poached" them from Australian

waters and Taiwanese dealers
subsequently undercut
Australian prices by a
considerable degree.

The shell is thick and very
heavy and, when taken live, is
covered with a brown
periostracum which later dries
and flakes off. Juvenile shells
have a complete tall spire and
apex often exceeding the length of
the body whorl and canal. The
spire breaks off and is never found
in mature shells.

Although a popular curio
among collectors, mainly on
account of its sheer size, little else
commends the species apart from
its graceful whorls. Its size has
made it useful to the Australian
Aborigines for carrying water.

1 *BUSYCON SPIRATUM* **Pear Whelk** *Lamarck 1816* (10cm/4in) *NE Caribbean* **C**. This thin, pyriform shell inhabits shallow water and has fine spiral lirae. The wavy lines on its grey-cream background colour vary from beige, through orange, to brown, and its aperture is stained yellow-orange.

2 *MELONGENA CORONA* **Common Crown Conch** *Gmelin 1791* (10cm/4in) *Caribbean* **C**. An attractive shell, found in mangroves. Its banding varies in coloration from cream to deep-brown-black on white. The edges of the shoulders are often spiny or coronated and axial growth scars are usually visible.

3 *BUSYCON CONTRARIUM* **Left-handed whelk** *Conrad 1840* (to

30cm/12in) *SE USA* **C**. A naturally sinistral species, this is a large, heavy shell which inhabits sand in shallow water.

4 *MELONGENA MELONGENA* **West Indian Crown Conch** *L. 1758* (to 15cm/6in) *Caribbean* **C**. A dweller in mud in intertidal, brackish water, this species is relatively smooth and is pyriform. Its coloration is dark brown with several cream spiral bands. In adult shells there are a few spines present on the whorl edges.

5 *BUSYCON CANALICULATUM* **Channelled Whelk** *L. 1758* (to 18cm/7in) *E USA* **C**. A lightweight shell with sharp, angled shoulders with deep sutures. The spire is low and the canal is fairly long. The aperture is yellowish.

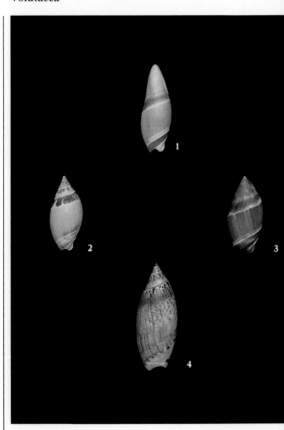

Olividae This group comprises several genera of mostly small and medium-sized shells with hard, very glossy surfaces, and many species are highly coloured. Olive shells and related genera are found in sand in all warm, shallow seas and are carnivorous night feeders.

1 *BARYSPIRA URASIMA* **Urasima Ancilla** *Kira 1955* (3.5cm/1¼in) *Japan and Taiwan* **C**. The spire is tall and heavily callused, especially on the ventral side. The slender body whorl is fawn with two orange-brown spiral bands.

2 *AMALDA MARGINATA* **Margin Ancilla** *Lamarck 1811* (to 4cm/1½in) *Australia* **U**. A shallow-water dweller with a medium-height spire and an inflated body whorl, around the lower part of which there are spiral grooves. It is an overall beige with brown axial banding around the shoulders.

3 *AMALDA AUSTRALIS* **Southern Ancilla** *Sowerby 1830* (3cm/1¼in) *New Zealand* **C**. A small, ovate species with a spire that is heavily callused down to the shoulder. The shell is brown with a broad, bluish band around the body whorl, and the interior is dark brown.

4 *AGARONIA TRAVASSOSI* **Travassos's Ancilla** *Morretes 1938* (5cm/2in) *Brazil* **U**. A tall, slender shell with a sharp apex, this species lives at depths of 25–150m (80–490ft). It is pale yellow with hazy spiral banding and many axial lines and zigzag markings. The aperture is creamy in colour.

1 *ANCILLA LIENARDI* **Lienardo's Ancilla** *Bernardi 1858* (to 5cm/2in) *Brazil* **U**. This stunning shell is vivid orange, thick, and highly glossy. The deep, open umbilicus is, like the aperture, white. It inhabits sand in shallow water.

2 *OLIVANCILLARIA SUBULATA* *Lamarck 1803* (7cm/2¾in) *Indonesia* **U**. The spire is high and pointed and the body whorl long and ovate. The shell is beige-yellow with fine cancellations and lines of brown. There are growth scars near the lip edge. The spire is usually callused.

3 *OLIVANCILLARIA URCEUS* **Bear Ancilla** *Röding 1798* (4cm/1½in) *E South America* **U**. The shell has a flat or depressed spire and a broad, angular body whorl. It is grey-beige with fine growth striae

in evidence. The columella and the area extending to the spire are heavily callused.

4 *ANCILLA VALESIANA* **Honey-banded Ancilla** *Iredale 1936* (to 9cm/3½in) *Australia* **C**. A shiny shell with a moderate, rich-red-brown spire and a rounded apex.

5 *OLIVANCILLARIA GIBBOSA* **Gibbose Olive** *Born 1778* (to 6cm/2½in) *Indian Ocean* **C**. A thick and heavy shell with a body whorl which is mottled greyish with an orange-brown spiral band on the lower third. There are fine growth lines. The columella is cream-white and callused, the callused area extending up to the narrow suture and on to the spire whorls. Specimens are sometimes yellow-orange.

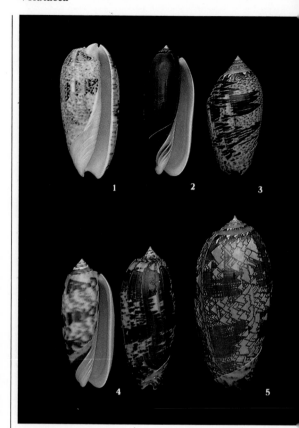

1 *OLIVA TEXTILINA* **Textile Olive** *Lamarck 1810* (to 10cm/ 4in) *SW Pacific* **C**. A large, thick species with a characteristic callus which rises at the top of the columella, above the whorl suture. The pattern is variable but generally there is a cream background with grey-brown wavy axial lines.

2 *OLIVA MINIACEA MARATTI Johnson 1871* (to 10cm/4in) *SW Pacific* **U**. Large, flawless specimens of this dark-brown, sometimes black, variant of *Oliva miniacea* are difficult to obtain.

3 *OLIVA INCRASSATA* **Angled Olive** *Lightfoot 1786* (to 9cm/3½in) *W Central America* **C**. This solid, heavy shell has an angled, thickened lip and is variable in colour, ranging from pure white to cream and yellow, with mottled and zigzag patterns in brown or cream.

4 *OLIVA MINIACEA* **Orange-mouthed olive** *Röding 1798* (to 10cm/4in) *Indo-Pacific* **C**. A large, heavy shell which lives in shallow water. The coloration is extremely variable, but the aperture is always orange.

5 *OLIVA PORPHYRIA* **Tent Olive** *L. 1758* (to 10cm/4in) *W Central America* **U**. The largest species of the genus and a handsome collectors' item, this shell inhabits sand in shallow water. It has a shkflort spire and plaited columella. The coloration is an overall violet-flesh tone and there are characteristic angular reticulations (tent markings) throughout.

1 *OLIVA BULOWI* **Bulow's Olive**
Sowerby 1888 (2cm/⅜in) *SW
Pacific* **U**. The shell is an overall
yellow with spiral wavy lines on
the lower part of the body whorl.
There is a fine suture.
2 *OLIVA CARNEOLA* **Carnelian
Olive** *Gmelin 1791* (1.5cm/⅝in)
Indo-Pacific **R**. Occasionally
fished in the Sulu Sea, this is the
albino form of the shell and is
most sought after by collectors.
3 *OLIVA CARNEOLA BIZONALIS
Dautzenberg 1927* (1.5cm/⅝in) *W
Pacific* **C**. A species with many
colour variations. The example
shown has two white bands on
orange.
4 *OLIVA TESSELLATA*
Tessellated Olive *Lamarck 1811*
(2.5cm/1in) *Indo-Pacific* **C**. A
pale-yellow shell with soft purple

spots. There is deep-purple
staining on the aperture and the
columella.
5 *OLIVA PARKINSONI*
Parkinson's Olive *Prior 1975*
(2cm/⅜in) *New Guinea* **U**. A pretty
shell with dark axial lines on the
spire and an angled ridge on the
shoulder.
6 *OLIVA DUCLOSI* **Duclos' Olive**
Reeve 1850 (2.5cm/1in) *Tahiti* **U**.
The spire is moderate, the body
whorl slightly inflated, and there
is dark tenting on a cream
background.
7 *OLIVA SIDELIA Duclos 1835*
(2.5cm/1in) *Indo-Pacific* **C**. The
shell has a depressed spire and a
body whorl with almost straight
sides. The pattern and coloration
are extremely variable and the
most usual form is shown here.

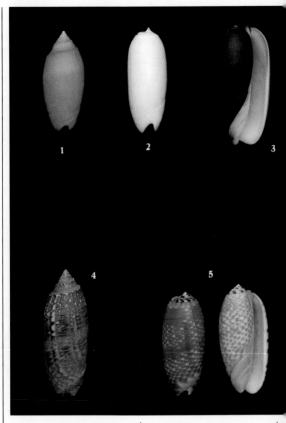

1

2

3

4

5

1 *OLIVA ANNULATA CARNICOLOR*
Blood Olive *Dautzenberg 1927*
(to 5cm/2in) *SW Pacific C.* The
spire is high and the body whorl is
inflated, with an angled shoulder.
There is a plaited columella. The
coloration is a beautiful peach-
orange.
2 *OLIVA LIGNARIA ALBESCENS*
Johnson 1914 (to 5cm/2in) *Sulu
Sea U.* This collectors' item is
variable and occurs in several
colour forms and subspecies. The
popular albino form is shown
here.
3 *OLIVA VIDUA Röding 1798* (to
6cm/2¼in) *Indo-Pacific C.* The
species has many colour forms
and subspecies. The chocolate-
brown form is shown here. The
aperture is white.
4 *OLIVA SAYANA* **Lettered Olive**

Ravenel 1834 (to 7cm/2¾in)
Caribbean C. The spire is raised,
with a deep suture, and there is a
plaited columella. The coloration
is cream-grey with brown zigzag
markings and there are often two
darker bands.
5 *OLIVA TRICOLOR* **Three-
coloured Olive** *Lamarck 1811*
(5cm/2in) *Indo-Pacific C.* An
attractive species showing
predominantly green spots and
splashes, with yellow and bluish
undertones on a cream
background.

1 *OLIVA RUBROLABIATA* **Red-lipped Olive** H. Fischer 1902 (4cm/1½in) *New Hebrides* **R**. The patterning is variable in this favourite among collectors, but the shell shown is typical.

2 *OLIVA BULBOSA* **Bulbous Olive** Röding 1798 (4cm/1½in) *Indian Ocean* **C**. One of the most variable species of the group, with several forms and subspecies, this shell ranges in colour from albino to dark-grey-brown. It is always solid and bulbous.

3 *OLIVA PERUVIANA FULGURATA* **Peruvian Olive** Martens 1869 (5cm/2in) *W South America* **C**. An attractive, thick, and heavy shell with a depressed spire and an angled shoulder.

4 *OLIVA MULTIPLICATA* Reeve 1850 (4.5cm/1¾in) *Japan and Taiwan* **U**.

This shell was commonly available in Taiwan but now appears to be difficult to obtain. It has an elegant, tall, slim spire and fine, dark tenting in the form of axial bands and, occasionally, broad spiral bands.

5 *OLIVA RUFULA* Duclos 1835 (3cm/1¼in) *SW Pacific* **C**. The markings on this shell are unusual but nonetheless fairly constant. It has a fawn background with broad, spiral, haphazard bands.

6 *OLIVA SPLENDIDULA* **Splendid Olive** Sowerby 1825 (to 5cm/2in) *W Central America* **U**. This attractive species rarely varies: the background is cream, with profuse tentings of brown and lavender, concentrated in two broad spiral bands. The columella is plaited.

Vasidae A small family of fairly large, solid shells, most of which live on coral reefs in tropical seas.
1 *VASUM TURBINELLUS* **Pacific Top Vase** *Lamarck 1822* (6cm/2¼in) *Indo-Pacific* **C**. This dweller in intertidal and shallow water has a medium spire with an angular and nodulose body whorl. There are long, curved spines on the shoulders and a row of smaller spines on the lower body whorl.
2 *VASUM CAPITELLUM* **Spined Caribbean Vase** *L. 1758* (6cm/2¼in) *Caribbean* **U**. A thick, coarse, reef-dwelling shell with a high spire and generally beige-brown in colour. There are strong spiral ridges towards the shoulders and the latter have blunt axial nodules.
3 *VASUM CASSIFORME* **Helmet**

Vase *Kiener 1841* (to 10cm/4in) *Brazil* **U**. A shallow-water species which is very coarsely spined and angular. The entire aperture area is a callused grey-brown.
4 *VASUM MURICATUM* **Caribbean Vase** *Born 1778* (7cm/2¾in) *Caribbean* **C**. This shallow-water species has a short, pointed spire and a very angular body whorl. The shell has spiral cords with blunt knobs on the shoulders.
5 *ALTIVASUM FLINDERSI* **Flinder's Vase** *Verco 1914* (to 15cm/6in) *W Australia* **U**. A superbly sculptured favourite among collectors, this shell is usually found dead, crabbed, often taken in cray pots from depths down to 300m (985ft). It ranges from white, through peach, to orange.

1 *VASUM TUBIFERUM* **Imperial Vase** *Anton 1839* (7cm/2¾in) *Philippines C.* A solid, coarsely ridged and spined shell, with long, upturned spines on the shoulders. This shallow-water species usually has an encrusted apex.

2 *TUDICULA ARMIGERA KURZI* **Kurz's Tudicula** *MacPherson 1963 N and W Australia U.* A beige and white shell with a tall spire, a rounded body whorl, and a long canal. It is very spinose, with long spines on the shoulders and the top part of the canal.

3 *TUDICULA INERMIS* **Toffee Apple Shell** *Angas 1878* (4cm/1½in) *N and W Australia U.* Similar in shape to *Tudicla spirillus* but much smaller and more rounded, this shell inhabits shallow waters. There are wavy

brown axial lines, a plaited white columella, spiral cording inside the aperture, and fine spiral striae.

4 *ALTIVASUM FLINDERSI* **Flinder's Vase** *Verco 1914* (10cm/4in) *S Australia U.* This, the form found in southern Australia, is much less spinose and is smaller than its western Australian counterpart. It is similarly variable in colour and is often taken alive.

5 *TUDICLA SPIRILLUS* **Spiral Tudicla** *L. 1767* (7cm/2¾in) *SE India C.* The species has a thick, rounded apex with a depressed spire and the body whorl is broad, inflated, and angled, with a long, curved siphonal canal. A shallow-water species, it has a callused parietal wall.

Turbinellidae Chank shells are
generally large and heavy and the
relatively few species are limited
to certain areas. They are often
referred to by the alternative
name *Xancus*.
1 *TURBINELLA ANGULATUS* **West
Indian Chank** *Lightfoot 1786*
(30cm/12in) *Caribbean* **C**. A very
large, heavy shell with strong,
blunt knobs on each whorl, a
columella with three plaits, and a
callused parietal area.

Harpidae Harp shells are among
the most beautiful of all shells.
Very popular with collectors, they
are highly glossy, small to
medium in size, and boast
exquisite patterns. They have
depressed spires and large,
inflated body whorls with distinct

axial folds or ribs. They are
mostly carnivorous and inhabit
shallow waters, often in corals or
sand. The family also includes the
genus *Morum*.
2 *HARPA COSTATA* **Imperial
Harp** *L. 1758* (to 9cm/3½in)
Mauritius **R**. A dweller in shallow
reef waters, this shell is restricted
in its range to Mauritius and the
immediate area. It has a flat spire
with a pinkish apex and an
enlarged body whorl with
numerous closely set ribs and
short, sharp spines on the
shoulder. The interior is yellow, as
is the columella, which also bears
two dark-brown blotches on the
upper part. Externally, there is
spiral banding of white, pale
brown, and pink and there are
often growth scars.

1 *HARPA CRENATA* **Crenate Harp** *Swainson 1822* (to 8cm/3¼in) *W Central America* **U.** This shell lacks the high gloss of the other species in the group and is a drab grey-pink with dark-brown blotches. The columella and parietal area are thinly callused. The species has an angular shoulder with a low spire, and there are eight or nine poorly formed axial ribs with fine zigzag markings between them. It inhabits shallow water.

2 *HARPA VENTRICOSA* **Ventral Harp** *Lamarck 1816* (8cm/3¼in) *E Africa* **C.** A thick, stout, shell with strong flattened and raised ribs. Pattern and colour are variable but there are usually spiral bands, axial loops, and zigzags of cream, pink, dark red, and brown, the pattern being rather angular. The species inhabits subtidal water.

3 *HARPA ARTICULARIS* **Articulate Harp** *Lamarck 1822* (9cm/3½in) *Indo-Pacific* **C.** A pretty shell with regular and distinctive blade-like axial ribs, each patterned spirally in pink and brown. The columella and parietal area are dark brown and glazed. Some pattern shows through to the interior, through the lip wall.

4 *HARPA MAJOR* **Major Harp** *Röding 1798* (to 10cm/4in) *Taiwan* **C.** A large, ovate, and fairly thin shell with widely spaced ribs. The spire is low and partially callused and the dark-brown columella is also callused. There are fine spiral markings of white, pink, and brown.

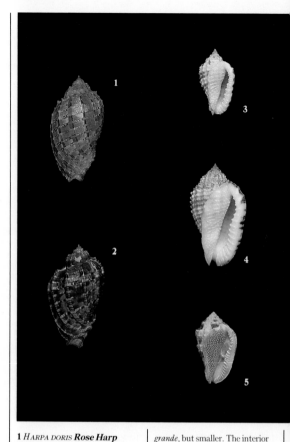

1 *HARPA DORIS* **Rose Harp**
Röding 1798 (6cm/2¼in) *W Africa*
U. Similar in its dull appearance
to *Harpa crenata*, this species is
more ovate. It is an overall pink-
brown with occasional red
blotches, a medium-height spire,
and indistinct, flat axial ribs.
2 *HARPA HARPA* **Noble Harp** *L.*
1758 (6cm/2¼in) *Indo-Pacific* **C**.
This smallish species has a fine
coloration. The axial ribs, which
are spiny on the shoulder, bear
spiral, black bands. The areas
between the ribs vary from pink
to deep-red-purple, with vague
patterns, and the interior is pale.
3 *MORUM CANCELLATUM*
Cancellate Morum *Sowerby*
1824 (4cm/1¾in) *Japan to Taiwan*
U. A deep-water species similar in
shape and sculpturing to *Morum*

grande, but smaller. The interior
is white.
4 *MORUM GRANDE* **Giant**
Morum *A. Adams 1855* (6cm/
2¼in) *Japan to Australia U*. The
largest species of the genus, this
shell inhabits deep water. It has
coarse spiral cords and the axial
ribs have short spines. The
aperture and parietal shield are
pure white.
5 *MORUM DENNISONI Reeve 1842*
(5cm/2in) *Caribbean* **R**. A much
sought-after species and a
favourite with collectors, this
shell is caught in trawler nets or
traps in very deep water. It has
spiral bands with blunt nodules
and dark-brown, haphazard,
axial bands and blotches. The
columella is orange with tiny
white pustules.

Mitridae A large, colourful family with many genera, the Mitres are mainly small to medium in size and fusiform. Some are smooth, while others are ridged or cancellate. They are carnivorous scavengers and inhabit warm, shallow water.

1 *MITRA BELCHERI* **Belcher's Mitre** *Hinds 1844* (12cm/4¾in) *W Central America* **U**. A large, handsome shell with flat spiral ribs and deep grooves. It is white or cream under a dark-brown periostracum and lives in shallow water.

2 *MITRA TEREBRALIS* **Auger-like Mitre** *Lamarck 1811* (10cm/4in) *Indo-Pacific* **U**. A rather narrow shell with a tall spire. There are fine, spiral, punctate grooves and the coloration is pale

orange with brown, flame-like axial stripes.

3 *MITRA MITRA* **Episcopal Mitre** *L. 1758* (to 12cm/4¾in) *Indo-Pacific* **C**. This, the largest of the Mitres, is an overall white or cream with rows of spiral dots or blotches of bright red. The surface is smooth and the columella is plaited.

4 *MITRA PAPALIS* **Papal Mitre** *L. 1758* (to 12cm/4¾in) *Indo-Pacific* **C**. An inhabitant of coral in shallow water, the shell is large and has a high spire. There are punctated spiral grooves on the first few whorls, the whorl shoulders are coronated, and the columella is plaited. The shell is white with spiral bands of deep-red-maroon spots or blotches.

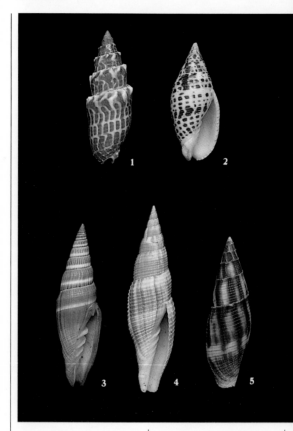

1 MITRA STICTICA **Pontifical
Mitre** Link 1807 (6cm/2¼in) *Indo-
Pacific C*. This striking reef
dweller is thick and has a high
spire with nodulose shoulders.
There are two rows of fine
punctations on each whorl. The
coloration is white with broad
axial and spiral squares and
blotches of pale red.

2 MITRA CARDINALIS **Cardinal
Mitre** Gmelin 1791 (7cm/2¾in)
Indo-Pacific C. A thick and heavy
shallow-water species with a high
spire and a rather broad body
whorl. The ground colour is white
and there are spiral rows of
broken spots and squares of red-
brown.

3 VEXILLUM COCCINEUM **Ornate
Mitre** Reeve 1844 (8cm/3⅛in)
Japan–Taiwan C. This tall,

narrow shallow-water dweller has
fine spiral lirae and fine axial ribs
on the early whorls. It is generally
orange with occasional thin white
or red-brown spiral banding.

4 CANCILLA ISABELLA **Isabelle's
Mitre** Swainson 1831 (9cm/3½in)
Japan–Taiwan U. A graceful
fusiform species which lives in
shallow water to a depth of 50m
(165ft). It is pale cream with
spiral grooves and axial threads.
The spire is tall.

5 MITRA EREMITARUM **Adusta
Mitre** Röding 1798 (6cm/2¼in) *SW
Pacific C*. This shell dwells on
intertidal reefs. It has a high spire,
coarse shoulder edges, and a
depressed suture. There are spiral
grooves and the columella is
plaited and the lip dentate.

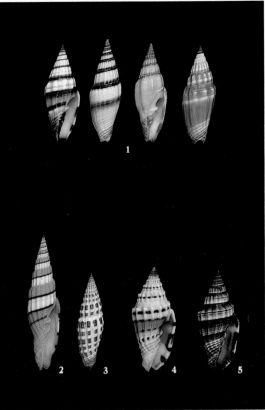

1 *VEXILLUM VULPECULA* **Little Fox Mitre** *L. 1758* (5cm/2in) *Indo-Pacific* *C*. An extremely variable patterned species, fusiform with a tall, pointed spire. An inhabitant of sand, the shell is cream with broad spiral bands of black, brown, orange, and yellow, and is sometimes even-coloured throughout.

2 *VEXILLUM CITRINUM* **Regal Mitre** *Gmelin 1791* (7cm/2¾in) *W Pacific* *U*. A beautifully patterned and variable shallow-water shell. It is tall and narrow with slight axial ribs.

3 *VEXILLUM STAINFORTHI* **Stainforth's Mitre** *Reeve 1841* (3cm/1¼in) *SW Pacific* *U*. A popular collectors' item, this fusiform shallow-water species has a high, pointed spire and is greyish with long, raised axial ribs which are streaked with red and yellow. The canal area and fasciole are blue-grey.

4 *VEXILLUM PLICARIUM* **Plicate Mitre** *L. 1758* (5cm/2in) *Indo-Pacific* *C*. This is a rather angular shell with a tall spire and with strong axial ribs bearing blunt nodules on the shoulders. There are fine and broad bands of blue-brown, orange, or near-black. It is found in sand in shallow water.

5 *VEXILLUM RUGOSUM* **Rugose Mitre** *Gmelin 1791* (5cm/2in) *Indo-Pacific* *C*. This sand dweller is short, coarsely sculptured, and has an angled body whorl. There are strong axial folds and fine spiral grooves and the surface has thin bands of black, brown, or grey. The interior is dark brown.

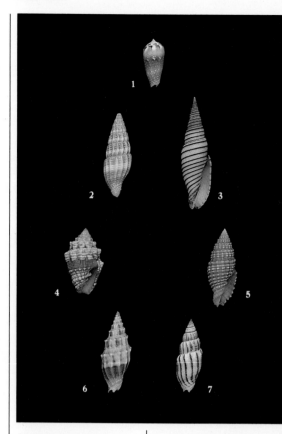

1 *IMBRICARIA VANIKORENSIS* **Vanikora Mitre** *Quoy and Gaimard 1833* (to 2cm/⅜in) *SW Pacific* **U**. A cone-shaped shell with a low spire and fine spiral grooves.

2 *VEXILLUM SCULPTILE Reeve 1845* (2.5cm/1in) *SW Pacific* **C**. This species has a high spire and fine, raised spiral ridges. There are alternate bands of creamy brown and white.

3 *CANCILLA PEASEI* **Pease's Mitre** *Dohrn 1860* (3.5cm/1⅓in) *SW Pacific* **U**. Tall and slender, with a high spire, this species is white and has fine, raised, brown spiral cords.

4 *VEXILLUM PATRIARCHALIS* **Patriarchal Mitre** *Gmelin 1791* (2.5cm/1in) *Indo-Pacific* **U**. This reef dweller is short, angular, and

coarsely sculptured, with spiral lirae and axial ribs, the latter nodulose on the shoulders.

5 *VEXILLUM CROCATUM* **Saffron Mitre** *Lamarck 1811* (2cm/⅞in) *Indo-Pacific* **U**. A small species with delicate spiral beading, this shell varies in colour from yellow to dark red. It lives in sand and coral rubble.

6 *VEXILLUM ECHINATUM* **Spiny Mitre** *A. Adams 1853* (2.5cm/1in) *Indo-Pacific* **C**. A beige-brown shell with fine spiral and axial beading. The shoulders have short, raised nodules.

7 *VEXILLUM EXASPERATUM Gmelin 1791* (2.5cm/1in) *Indo-Pacific* **C**. This pretty shell is found on coral reefs and has very fine spiral cords and raised axial ribs streaked with brown.

Volutidae This large family is very popular with collectors since the shells, although lacking detailed sculpturing, are often highly patterned and colourful. They live mainly in tropical seas, in shallow to very deep water, and all species are carnivorous.

1 *CYMBIOLA MAGNIFICA* **Magnificent Volute** *Gebauer 1802* (to 25cm/10in) *E Australia* **C**. An inhabitant of sand at depths down to 100m (330ft), this shell has a short spire and a large, ovate body whorl which occasionally has blunt knobs on the shoulder. The base colour is pinkish-white, with brown zig-zag markings, and the interior is flesh-coloured.

2 *LIVONIA MAMILLA* **Mammal Volute** *Sowerby 1844* (25cm/10in) *Australia* **U**. A large and ovate shell with a prominent, rounded protoconch. The spire is low and the body whorl is inflated.

3 *CYMBIUM GLANS* **Elephant Snout** *Gmelin 1791* (to 30cm/12in) *W Africa* **C**. A large, heavy, and aptly named shallow-water species. The spire is sunken and callused and the shoulder is sharp and curves outwards. The aperture is oval and gaping and the lip is rarely smooth. Grains of sand are frequently trapped under the glazed covering of the beige-brown exterior.

4 *MELO AETHIOPICA* **Ethiopian Melon** *L. 1758* (25cm/10in) *SW Pacific* **C**. This large, heavy, offshore species has a flat spire and regular triangular spines on the shoulders.

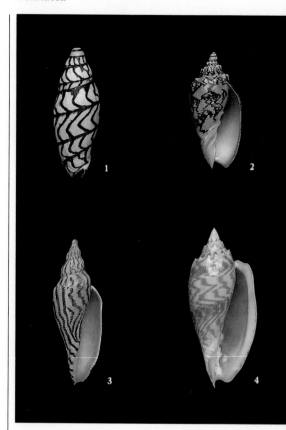

1 *VOLUTOCONUS BEDNALLI*
Bednall's Volute *Brazier 1878*
(to 12cm/4¾in) *N Australia* **R**. This
choice collectors' item is robust
and thick and has a rounded,
swollen spire. There are fine axial
striae and the columella has
strong plaits. The coloration is
cream, with a distinct lattice-
work of dark brown. It is found
on sand at 10–50m (35–165ft).
2 *CYMBIOLA VESPERTILIO* **Bat
Volute** *L. 1758* (to 10cm/4in) *SW
Pacific* **C**. The species is found in
mud in shallow water and varies
in size, shape, and pattern. It is
very glossy, with a moderate spire
and an inflated body whorl.
Nodules on the shoulder are
sometimes extended into
upturned points.
3 *FULGORARIA RUPESTRIS* **Asian**

Flame Volute *Gmelin 1791*
(11cm/4¼in) *Japan–Taiwan* **C**. A
species of deep, offshore waters,
this shell has a high spire, a
rounded protoconch, axial ribs on
the early whorls, and fine spiral
lirae. Growth scars are evident
and the lip is dentate. The
coloration is cream-beige with
strong, brown, wavy axial lines.
4 *CYMBIOLISTA HUNTERI*
Hunter's Volute *Iredale 1931*
(13cm/5in) *E Australia* **C**. A
dweller in shallow to fairly deep
water, this shell is quite large but
light, and has a flaring, extended
lip. It is smooth, with small, sharp
nodules on the whorl shoulders. It
is often pale cream with fine, blue-
brown axial stripes, or, like the
deep-water specimen shown here,
displays deep-orange markings.

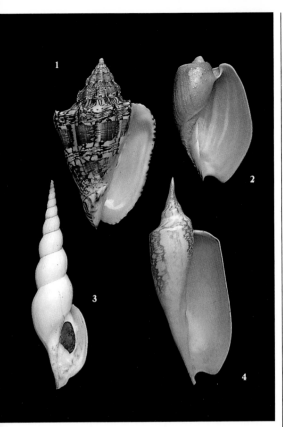

1 *VOLUTA EBRAEA* **Hebrew Volute** *L. 1758* (to 15cm/6in) *Brazil* **C**. This strikingly patterned, robust, and thick shell varies in colour and size. The spire is moderate and the body whorl angular. Rounded axial ribs extend to sharp points at the shoulder. The species inhabits shallow water.

2 *CYMBIUM OLLA* **Olla Volute** *L. 1758* (10cm/4in) *NW Africa* **C**. An inhabitant of depths of 50–100m (165–330ft), this species has a short, rounded spire above a wide, depressed suture. A rounded, level shoulder extends to the inflated body whorl. The aperture is wide and gaping. The shell is beige, with growth scars, and occasionally grains of sand are trapped beneath the glaze.

3 *TEREMACHIA DUPREYAE* **Duprey's Volute** *Emerson 1985* (to 18cm/7in) *NW Australia* **R**. A thin, light shell with a very tall and graceful spire. The whorls are rounded and the canal is short. There are fine axial striae on the early whorls. An inhabitant of depths of 300–500m (985–1640ft), the shell has only in recent years become available in any numbers.

4 *ZIDONA DUFRESNEI* **Angular Volute** *Donovan 1823* (15cm/6in) *Brazil and Argentina* **U**. The spire is moderate in height but narrow, pointed, and curved, and the wide, angled shoulder extends to a long body whorl. Almost all the shell, and particularly the spire, is covered with a fine, callused glaze. The shell lives at depths of 40–80m (130–260ft).

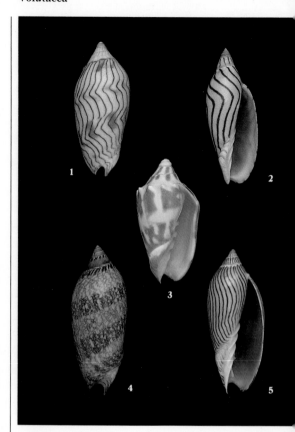

1 *AMORIA UNDULATA* **Wavy Volute** *Lamarck 1804* (9cm/3½in) *S Australia* **C**. A thick, heavy, porcellaneous shell with undulating axial lines on a cream or beige background. The interior is pale orange.

2 *AMORIA KAWAMURAI* **Kawamura's Volute** *Habe 1975* (10cm/4in) *Japan–Taiwan* **R**. This smooth, highly glossy, and fusiform shell has a low, pointed spire and an ovate body whorl. It is cream, with vivid, wavy axial stripes, orange staining around the latter stages of the suture, and an orange interior.

3 *CYMBIOLA DESHAYESI* **Deshayes's Volute** *Reeve 1855* (9cm/3½in) *New Caledonia* **U**. A stout, heavy species, this shallow-water dweller has a moderate

spire with a rounded protoconch. The body whorl is angled and the shoulders are nodulose. There are two broad bands of broken deep-orange blotches on a cream base.

4 *AMORIA DAMONII* **Damon's Volute** *Gray 1864* (10cm/4in) *Australia* **C**. A shallow-water dweller which is highly glossy and variable in pattern. It is generally grey-beige, with few or many fine, brown, triangular reticulations, concentrated into two or three brown, spiral bands.

5 *AMORIA ELLIOTI* **Elliot's Volute** *Sowerby 1864* (8cm/3½in) *W Australia* **U**. Found at low tide in sand, this species has a rather inflated, fusiform shape and a low spire. It is beige, with many fine, wavy axial stripes and a deeply plaited columella.

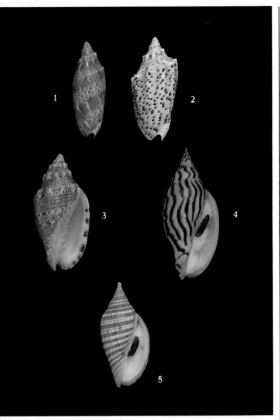

1 *CYMBIOLACCA CRACENTA*
Graceful Volute *McMichael
1963* (7cm/2¾in) *NE Australia* **U**.
A slender, highly glossy, shallow-water shell of an overall pink with broad, brick-red bands and small axial dots and dashes. The columella and interior are white and there are sharp nodules on the shoulder.

2 *CYMBIOLACCA PERISTICTA*
Spotted Volute *McMichael 1963*
(7cm/2¾in) *NE Australia* **U**. A shallow-water species, creamy-white, highly glossy, and with many small, dark-red-brown dots and dashes. The spire is moderate and the inflated body whorl has short, sharp nodules on the shoulder.

3 *VOLUTA MUSICA* **Music Volute**
L. 1758 (to 8cm/3¼in) *Caribbean* **U**.

A robust, thick, and highly patterned shell varying from pink, through orange, to slate grey. All shells have spiral rows and bands of dots, lines, and squares resembling medieval musical notation. This shallow-water dweller occurs in several variants and subspecies.

4 *VOLUTA LOROISI* **Lorois's
Volute** *Valenciennes 1863* (8cm/3¼in) *S India and Sri Lanka* **U**. An offshore species, this shell has a high spire and an inflated body whorl.

5 *HARPULINA ARAUSIACA*
Vexillate Volute *Lightfoot 1786*
(7cm/2¾in) *S India and Sri Lanka*
R. This collectors' favourite is fusiform and its spire is moderate, with a rounded protoconch. It is a shallow-water dweller.

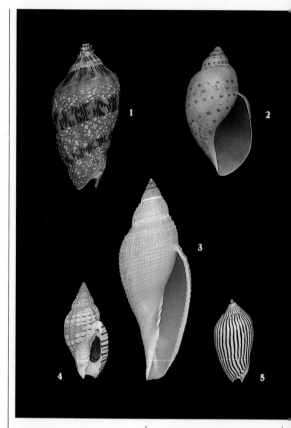

1 *CYMBIOLA NIVOSA* **Snowy Volute** Lamarck 1804 (8cm/3¼in) W Australia **C**. A shallow-water species which is an overall grey-brown with spiral bands and many white dots and blotches. The columella is orange. The spire is moderate, with a rounded apex, and the body whorl is inflated.

2 *AMPULLA PRIAMUS* **Spotted Flask** Gmelin 1791 (6cm/2½in) NE Atlantic **U**. A thin, light, and bulbous shell with rounded whorls. It is dull beige-orange, with spiral bands of broken brown dots and dashes, and lives at depths of 50–300m (65–985ft).

3 *VOLUTOCORBIS ABYSSICOLA* **Abyssal Volute** Adams and Reeve 1850 (to 11cm/4¼in) South Africa **U**. Occurring at depths down to 500m (1640ft), this species is very fusiform and has a high spire. It has spiral beading and axial lirae. The lip is dentate and the columella and parietal area are glazed.

4 *LYRIA DELESSERTIANA TULEARENSIS* Cosel and Blöcher 1977 (5cm/2in) Madagascar **U**. This thick fusiform shell has strong axial ribs with fine spiral lines on orange bands. The aperture is white and there are strong black lines on the edge of the lip. The whorls are rounded.

5 *AMORIA ZEBRA* **Zebra Volute** Leach 1814 (to 5cm/2in) Australia **C**. This shell is cream with vivid brown axial stripes, although all-yellow or all-brown varieties occur. The spire is short and the body whorl is ovate.

Marginellidae A large family popular with collectors and found worldwide in warm water, the Margins are mostly small, glossy, and very colourful.

1 *MARGINELLA GLABELLA* **Shiny Margin** L. *1758* (4cm/1½in) *NW Africa* **C**. This inhabitant of shallow water to a depth of 75m (245ft) is highly glossy and fusiform and has an inflated body whorl. It is basically pink-orange, with white spots and blotches, but the patterning is variable.

2 *MARGINELLA ELEGANS* **Elegant Margin** *Gmelin 1791* (4cm/1½in) *Andaman Sea* **C**. Similar in shape to *Marginella strigata*, this shell is pale grey with fine, dark, spiral bands broken by pale axial lines. It lives on sand in shallow water.

3 *MARGINELLA STRIGATA* **Striped Margin** *Dillwyn 1817* (4cm/1½in) *Andaman Sea* **C**. A grey shell with dark, zigzag, axial lines and a thick, pale-orange lip. This shallow-water dweller has a flat spire and a large aperture.

4 *MARGINELLA SEBASTIANI* **Sebastian's Margin** *Marche and Rosso 1979* (6cm/2¼in) *W Africa* **U**. Pale-peach-brown with spiral bands of white dots and squares, this ovate shell was formerly confused with *Marginella goodalli*.

5 *MARGINELLA BULLATA* **Bubble Margin** *Born 1778* (7cm/2¾in) *Brazil* **U**. Found on sand or gravel in shallow water, this species has a flat, callused spire and a large, tapering body whorl. The lip is thickened.

1 *MARGINELLA MOSAICA* **Mosaic Margin** *Sowerby 1846* (2.5cm/1in) *South Africa* **R**. Often collected dead from the beach, this shell has a low spire, an angled body whorl, and a thickened lip.
2 *PERSICULA LILACINA* **Lilac Margin** *Sowerby 1846* (to 3cm/1¼in) *Brazil* **R**. An offshore species with a flat or sunken spire and an inflated body whorl. This shell is pale grey, with three broad, darker bands and a pinkish, thickened lip.
3 *PERSICULA CINGULATA* **Girdled Margin** *Dillwyn 1817* (1cm/½in) *W Africa* **C**. This dweller in sand or mud has a flat or sunken spire and an inflated body whorl.
4 *PERSICULA PERSICULA* **Spotted Margin** *L. 1758* (2cm/¾in) *W*

Africa **C**. This shallow-water dweller is similar in shape to *Persicula cingulata* and is fawn, with many brown spots.
5 *MARGINELLA PSEUDOFABA* **Queen Margin** *Sowerby 1846* (4cm/1½in) *W Africa* **R**. A deep-water species with a moderate spire and an angled body whorl. There are axial nodules on the spire and the shoulder and the coloration is white and grey with black dots.
6 *PRUNUM LABIATA* **Royal Margin** *Kiener 1841* (4cm/1½in) *Central America and Caribbean* **U**. This shell is pink-peach, with a thickened, yellow-tinted lip. It has an inflated, tapering body whorl and a short, callused spire and is found in sand in low-tide areas.

Cancellariidae Nutmeg shells
form a pretty group, for, despite
their dull coloration, they have
attractive, delicate sculpturing
and shapes. They inhabit sand in
tropical seas.
1 *CANCELLARIA LYRATA* **Lyrate
Nutmeg** *Brocchi 1814* (4cm/1½in)
W Africa **R**. A subtidal species
with a tall spire and sharp, raised
axial ribs and prominent varices.
The shell is beige and there are
white, spiral bands bearing short,
sharp spines on each rib around
the centre of the whorl.
2 *CANCELLARIA NODULIFERA*
Knobbed Nutmeg *Sowerby 1825*
(to 5cm/2in) *Japan* **U**. This
shallow-water shell is beige and
coarsely sculptured with spiral
cords and axial, nodulose ribs.
3 *CANCELLARIA CANCELLATA*

Cancellate Nutmeg *L. 1767* (to
4cm/1½in) *W Africa* **C**. This shell
has a moderate spire and an
inflated body whorl. There are
strong axial ribs and spiral cords
and the aperture and columella
are white. The shell is found in
shallow water.
4 *CANCELLARIA SPENGLERIANA*
Spengler's Nutmeg *Deshayes
1830* (to 6cm/2¼in) *Japan* **C**. This
shallow-water species is solid and
has a tall spire. There are strong
axial ribs and spiral cording, and
blunt nodules on the shoulders.
5 *CANCELLARIA CASSIDIFORMIS*
Helmet Nutmeg *Sowerby 1832*
(4cm/1½in) *W Central America* **C**.
A solid and inflated shell with a
low spire, nodulose shoulders, and
fine spiral and axial cording. It
has a white, lirate aperture.

133

1 *CANCELLARIA OBLONGA*
Oblong Nutmeg *Sowerby 1825*
(3cm/1¼in) *Indian Ocean* ***U***. This
offshore species is fusiform, with a
moderate spire, and is yellow
beige with broad brown bands. It
has fine axial and spiral beading.
2 *CANCELLARIA TESSELLATA*
Tessellated Nutmeg *Sowerby
1832* (3cm/1¼in) *W Central
America* ***U***. A white, beige, and
grey shell with a short spire and
an inflated, ovate body whorl. It
has fine axial and spiral cords and
the thickened lip, columella, and
parietal area are white.
3 *CANCELLARIA PISCATORIA*
Fisherman's Nutmeg *Gmelin
1791* (to 3cm/1¼in) *W Africa* ***U***.
The spire is short and the body
whorl globose in this grey-beige,
shallow-water dweller. It has

spiral beading and fine axial ribs
which are nodulose at the
shoulders. The aperture has a
white rim.
4 *TRIGONOSTOMA PELLUCIDA*
Triangular Nutmeg *Perry 1811*
(2.5cm/1in) *SW Pacific* ***R***. A
beige, shallow-water dweller with
a high spire and wide-angled
shoulders, which together give it
the look of a pagoda. There are
fine axial ribs, minutely nodulose,
which rise to short, sharp spines
on the shoulders. The umbilicus is
deep and wide.
5 *SCALPTIA MERCADOI*
Mercado's Nutmeg *Old 1968*
(3cm/1¼in) *Philippines* ***R***. An
offshore species, this shell has a
high spire and rounded whorls. It
has very thick, incised axial ribs
and spiral lirae.

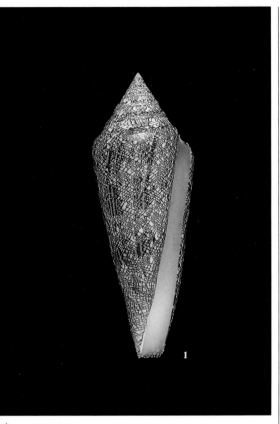

1

Conidae Cone shells are one of the most popular of groups, partly because of the vast variety of patterns and colours and the diversity of the basic conical shape. There are hundreds of species, and new species and forms are constantly added to the list.

All species are carnivorous and most inhabit shallow waters between reefs and the shore. They all have a periostracum which hides the patterns beneath. Many are highly poisonous and have proved fatal to humans.
1 *CONUS GLORIAMARIS* **Glory of the Sea Cone** *Chemnitz* 1777 (to 13cm/5in) *Philippines* **U**.
Possibly the most famous and sought after of all shells, very few specimens were possessed in the 18th and 19th centuries and those only by the wealthy. Almost none were collected during the first half of this century, but the shell has been fished in ever-greater numbers since the 1950s so that now its status is uncommon rather than very rare (although this classification is debatable).

Although it is not particularly beautiful compared with other species, this shell has an elegant, tapering body whorl and a moderate spire with a rounded shoulder. The coloration is generally brown-olive-green on white and there are minute tent markings throughout. *Conus gloriamaris* belongs to the highly toxic "Textile" group and live specimens should be handled with great care.

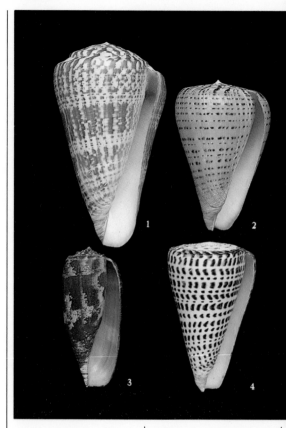

1 *CONUS PULCHER* **Butterfly Cone** *Lightfoot 1786* (to 18cm/7in) *W Africa* **U.** The largest of the Cones, this shallow-water dweller is thick and heavy, with a low or flattened spire and a large, angled, typically conical body whorl. Large, perfect specimens are difficult to obtain.

2 *CONUS BETULINUS* **Beech Cone** *L. 1758* (to 12cm/4¾in) *Indo-Pacific* **C.** A large and heavy species with a flat spire with a small, raised apex and an inflated, tapering body whorl. It inhabits shallow water.

3 *CONUS GEOGRAPHUS* **Geography Cone** *L. 1758* (to 13cm/5in) *Indo-Pacific* **C.** Large and light, with a low spire, this shell has nodulose shoulders and a long, slightly tapering body

whorl. The aperture is wide, particularly at the anterior end. The background is pinkish, with large bands and areas of red-brown. There are a few fine tent markings between the bands and the shell is glossy overall. The species has a highly poisonous sting, which can be fatal.

4 *CONUS LEOPARDUS* **Leopard Cone** *Röding 1798* (13cm/5in) *Indo-Pacific* **C.** An inhabitant of shallow water, this is a thick, heavy species with a flat spire which is usually encrusted or eroded. The body whorl is sharply angled, tapering, and conical. The coloration is creamy white with spiral rows of blue-grey vertical lines and dots. Large shells usually have filed lips, unless taken *in situ*.

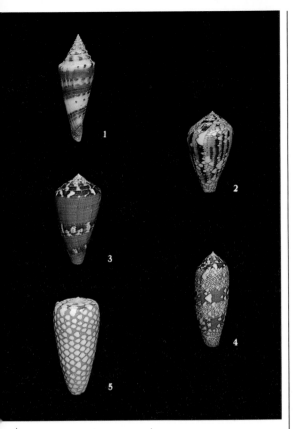

1 CONUS ICHINOSEANA **Ichinose Cone** *Kuroda 1956* (6cm/2¼in) *Japan to Philippines **U**.* A very light, thin shell with a long body whorl and a high, raised spire. Brown banding on a white background characterizes this deepwater shell.

2 CONUS RETIFER **Netted Cone** *Menke 1829* (to 4cm/1½in) *Indo-Pacific **U**.* A thick, pyriform shell which is beautifully patterned with axial bands of black, orange, and white spiral tent marks. It is fairly glossy and inhabits shallow water.

3 CONUS VITTATUS **Ribboned Cone** *Hwass 1792* (3cm/1¼in) *W Central America **U**.* This offshore dweller has a solid shell with a moderate spire and a tapering, rather convex body whorl. It has

fine, spiral lirae with variable colours – brown, orange and pink, and one or two broad patterned bands and a brown and white spire.

4 CONUS AURICOMUS **Gold Leafed Cone** *Hwass 1792* (to 5cm/2in) *Indo-Pacific **U**.* This long, cylindrical shell, tapering at the anterior end, with a low, convex spire is prettily netted with beige-brown on white. It dwells on coral reefs.

5 CONUS NOBILIS **Noble Cone** *L. 1758* (4cm/1½in) *W Pacific **U**.* An elegant and delicately patterned shell with a virtually flat spire and slightly convex sides. This glossy, mustard-coloured shell has white tent markings.

137

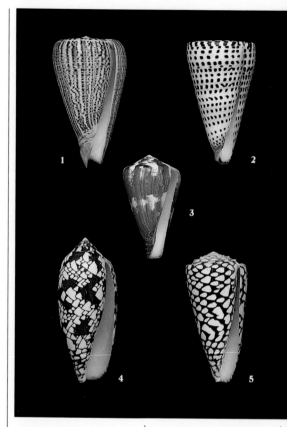

1 *CONUS BETULINUS SURATENSIS*
Hwass 1792 (10cm/4in) *C.* Similar
to *Conus betulinus* but this flat-
spired shell has very fine axial
lines of broken dots and small
blotches. The siphonal canal is
tinted with orange.

2 *CONUS LITTERATUS* **Lettered
Cone** *L. 1758* (to 10cm/4in) *Indo-
Pacific C.* A glossy, fairly large,
and heavy shell similar to *Conus
leopardus*, but with faint pale-
yellow spiral bands beneath the
rows of black dots or squares. The
spire is flat, even depressed. The
species lives in intertidal and
shallow water.

3 *CONUS VEXILLUM* **Flag Cone**
Gmelin 1791 (to 10cm/4in) *Indo-
Pacific C.* A solid offshore dweller
with a low-angled spire and a
sharply angled body whorl, this

shell is glossy and some examples
resemble polished wood. It often
has broad bands of white on a
ground colour which ranges from
orange to brown.

4 *CONUS AULICUS* **Princely Cone**
L. 1758 (to 13cm/5in) *Indo-Pacific
U.* A beautiful species and very
popular with collectors. The spire
is low-angled and the body whorl
is rather inflated and convex. It is
glossy and vividly patterned. This
highly venomous species inhabits
coral reefs.

5 *CONUS MARMOREUS* **Marble
Cone** *L. 1758* (to 11cm/4½in) *Indo-
Pacific C.* A large, heavy and
attractive shell with a very low
coronated spire and a gently
tapering body whorl. It dwells in
sandy, shallow water.

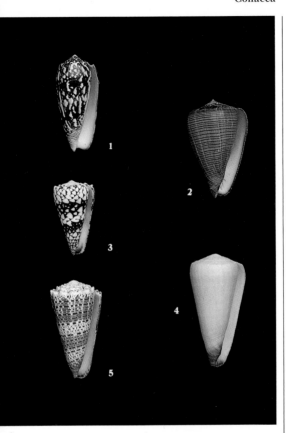

1 *CONUS STRIATUS* **Striated
Cone** *L. 1758* (10cm/4in) *Indo-
Pacific* *C.* The shell has a silky
sheen and most often a white
background, with brown, blue-
grey, or black markings, although
the colour and patterning are
variable. There are very fine
spiral striae. The body whorl is
cylindrical and the upper part
rather inflated. The spire is short
and stepped. This species is
venomous.
2 *CONUS FIGULINUS* **Fig Cone** *L.
1758* (to 8cm/3¼in) *Indo-Pacific* *C.*
A rich-brown, rather shiny shell
with fine spiral lirae. It is heavy,
with a low, concave spire and
slightly inflated sides. The
aperture is white and the shell is
found in shallow water.
3 *CONUS MARMOREUS BANDANUS*

Banded Marble Cone *Hwass
1792* (8cm/3¼in) *E Africa* *C.* This
shell is similar to *Conus
marmoreus*, but is generally
shorter and has three distinct
spiral bands of large white tent
markings on a black base colour.
4 *CONUS VIRGO* **Virgin Cone** *L.
1758* (to 9cm/3½in) *Indo-Pacific* *C.*
This sand dweller has an almost
flat spire and a long, straight-
sided, and tapering body whorl.
5 *CONUS IMPERIALIS* **Imperial
Cone** *L. 1758* (to 9cm/3½in) *Indo-
Pacific* *C.* A solid, heavy, and
handsome reef dweller, this shell
has a coronated spire and a
straight-sided body with spiral
broken lines, dots, or dashes. It is
variable in colour, but is often
white, with a broad beige-orange
background coloration.

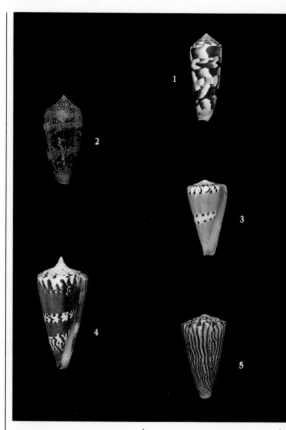

1 *CONUS GUBERNATOR* **Governor Cone** *Hwass 1792* (7cm/2¾in) *E Africa* **C**. This shallow-water dweller is an attractive and variable shell. It is tall, with a low, stepped spire and is cylindrical, with gently tapering sides.
2 *CONUS EUETRIOS Sowerby 1882* (7cm/2¾in) *E Africa* **U**. Only recently available, this pretty species has an overall blue-grey background with large areas of broken brown banding. There are fine tent markings and the aperture is pale grey. The spire is moderate and concave, the body whorl convex.
3 *CONUS MUSTELINUS* **Weasel Cone** *Hwass 1792* (6cm/2¼in) *Indo-Pacific* **C**. Not to be confused with *Conus capitaneus*, this shell has a low, almost flat,

spire with a rounded shoulder and straight sides.
4 *CONUS GENERALIS* **General Cone** *L. 1767* (to 8cm/3¼in) *Indo-Pacific* **C**. A handsome, variable species with a sharp, often high, concave spire and straight, tapering sides. This intertidal dweller is orange or brown and there are broad bands of broken white with dark axial streaks.
5 *CONUS PRINCEPS* **Prince Cone** *L. 1758* (7cm/2¾in) *Central W America* **U**. A popular collectors' shell, handsomely marked with black axial streaks on a deep-orange background. The shoulder is nodulose and there are spiral ridges on the lower part of the body whorl. It lives in shallow water.

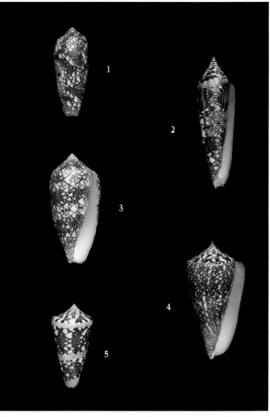

1 *CONUS PENNACEUS* **Feathered Cone** *Born 1778* (6cm/2¼in) *Indo-Pacific C*. This shell has a low to flat spire and a cylindrical body which is slightly inflated at the shoulder. Its coloration varies.
2 *CONUS BENGALENSIS* **Bengal Cone** *Okatuni 1968* (10cm/4in) *Bay of Bengal R*. This much-prized collectors' item has a tall, elegant body and a moderate spire. It is richly ornamented, with white tenting and wide spiral bands of orange-brown. It lives in deep water in a restricted range.
3 *CONUS TEXTILE* **Textile Cone** *L. 1758* (to 10cm/4in) *Indo-Pacific C*. A very beautiful species with a short, angled spire and a convex body whorl. It is entirely covered with white tenting and spiral bands of orange and brown. There

are several varieties and subspecies of this venomous shallow-water dweller.
4 *CONUS AMADIS Gmelin 1791* (8cm/3¼in) *Indian Ocean C*. An offshore dweller, this shell has a moderate, concave spire and a straight-sided, tapering body whorl. The coloration varies from albino, through yellow, to dark brown, with bands of different-sized tent markings.
5 *CONUS AMMIRALIS* **Admiral Cone** *L. 1758* (6cm/2¼in) *Indo-Pacific U*. This species lives in sand or corals. It has a low spire and a straight-sided body richly ornamented with broad crimson-brown bands and yellow-gold tent markings. It is rarely pustulose. The shell has become rather difficult to obtain in recent years.

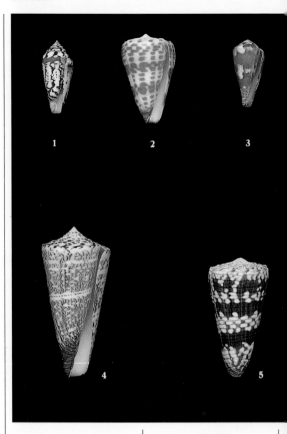

1

2

3

4

5

1 *CONUS ALGOENSIS SIMPLEX Sowerby 1857* (3cm/1¼in) *South Africa* **U**. A species with variable patterning, this shell is pale-cream-grey, with brown, wavy, axial streaks and spots and sometimes a broad spiral band. An inhabitant of shallow water, it has a moderate spire with rounded shoulders and straight sides.

2 *CONUS TESSULATUS* **Tessellated Cone** *Born 1778* (5cm/2in) *Indo-Pacific* **C**. A small, stocky shell with a low spire and a straight-sided body whorl, this species is found in shallow water. It is white, with orange-red spiral bands of broken squares, and the anterior end has a lavender tip.

3 *CONUS PERTUSUS* **Pertusus Cone** *Hwass 1792* (to 6cm/2¼in) *Indo-Pacific* **U**. A pinkish shell, with two broad, white, spiral bands and some axial streaks. Deep-coloured specimens are much sought-after by collectors.

4 *CONUS THALASSIARCHUS* **Bough Cone** *Sowerby 1834* (8cm/3¼in) *Philippines* **C**. This shallow-water dweller is beige-orange to black on a cream background and has variable markings, although these are usually spiral bands of lines, dots, and streaks.

5 *CONUS ZONATUS* **Zoned Cone** *Hwass 1792* (7cm/2¾in) *S India to Indonesia* **U**. The spire is low and coronated and the body whorl has straight sides. The coloration is white, with fine, brown spiral lines and wide, broken bands or patches of slate-grey-blue.

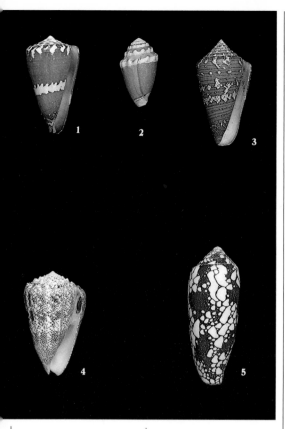

1 *CONUS LITHOGLYPHUS*
Lithograph Cone *Hwass 1792*
(5cm/2in) *Indo-Pacific* *C.* This
shell has a flat spire and a narrow,
straight-sided body. It is pale-
orange or brown, with a central
white band and there are white
spots on the shoulder.
2 *CONUS DORREENSIS* **Pontifical
Cone** *Péron 1807* (3cm/1¼in) *W
Australia* *C.* A thick, short shell
which lives in shallow water. It is
cream, with a pale-green-brown
periostracum.
3 *CONUS CEDO-NULLI* **Matchless
Cone** *L. 1767* (5cm/2in) *Caribbean
R.* A much-prized shallow-water
species, this shell has a moderate,
stepped spire and straight sides.
It is an overall mid-brown, with
spiral rows of black and white
dots. There are larger central

areas of axial cream-white
splashes. Rarely, the shell is
orange or lavender.
4 *CONUS ARENATUS* **Sand-
dusted Cone** *Hwass 1792* (to
6cm/2½in) *Indo-Pacific* *C.* A
shallow-water dweller, this heavy
shell has a low, coronated spire
and a slightly convex body. There
are many small, dark flecks on a
cream background, and two
broad, spiral bands are often
found.
5 *CONUS EPISCOPUS* **Episcopal
Cone** *Hwass 1792* (8cm/3¼in)
Indo-Pacific *C.* Similar to *Conus
pennaceus*, but with a rather
longer and more rounded spire
and shoulder, this shell has large,
white tent markings on brown.

1 *CONUS AUGUR* **Augur Cone**
Lightfoot 1786 (6cm/2¼in) *E Africa*
U. The spire is flat and the sides
are founded in this coral-reef
dweller. It is cream, with fine,
spiral rows of dots and two broad
bands of broken, dark-brown
squares and blotches.
2 *CONUS ORBIGNYI* **Orbigny's**
Cone *Audouin 1831* (7cm/2¾in) *W*
Pacific U. A tall, slender species
with a raised, angled spire and a
concave body whorl. It has raised
spiral cords with broken brown
dashes and is fished in deep water.
3 *CONUS GENUANUS* **Garter**
Cone *L. 1758* (to 6cm/2¼in) *W*
Africa C. A handsome shallow-
water dweller with a low-angled
spire and a straight-sided body
whorl. The coloration is pale
lavender with vivid spiral bands

of blue-black dots, dashes, and
blotches.
4 *CONUS EBRAEUS* **Hebrew Cone**
L. 1758 (4cm/1½in) *Indo-Pacific C*.
A small, chunky shell with a low,
rounded spire and convex sides. A
shallow-water species, it is
smooth and shiny and its
coloration is cream-white with
vivid black spiral bands of
squares and streaks.
5 *CONUS BARTHELEMYI*
Bartholomew's Cone *Bernardi*
1861 (6cm/2¼in) *Reunion Islands*
U. This choice collectors' item has
a low, stepped spire and a
straight-sided body whorl. An
offshore species, it is deep-orange,
with broken spiral bands of black
and white in blotches and spots.
There are spiral grooves above the
anterior end of the body whorl.

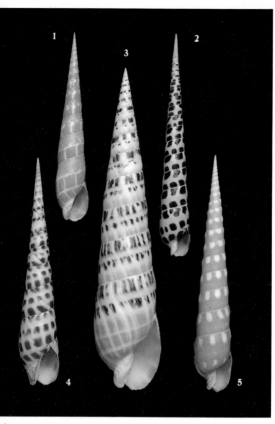

Terebridae The Augers are long, slender shells with very tall spires and are smooth or sculptured, with narrow apertures and short canals. They live in warm seas, generally in shallow water, and are carnivorous.

1 *TEREBRA DIMIDIATA* **Dimidiate Auger** *L. 1758* (to 12cm/4¾in) *Indo-Pacific C.* This shell is of moderate size, with about 16 whorls, and is pink-orange with cream axial streaks. There is a spiral groove on the upper part of each whorl.

2 *TEREBRA SUBULATA* **Subulate Auger** *L. 1767* (13cm/5in) *Indo-Pacific C.* A strikingly marked shell of medium size with a minimum of 20 whorls.

3 *TEREBRA MACULATA* **Marlinspike Auger** *L. 1758*
(20cm/8in) *Indo-Pacific C.* A heavy shell, the largest of the genus. It is mostly smooth, with a very tall spire of at least 16 whorls. The coloration is cream, with beige spiral bands, dark axial streaks and blotches, and fine axial growth lines.

4 *TEREBRA AREOLATA* **Muscaria uger** *Link 1807* (13cm/5in) *Indo-Pacific C.* A medium-sized shell with at least 15 whorls. The coloration is cream, with three spiral bands of squares or blotches of brown on each whorl.

5 *TEREBRA GUTTATA* **Spotted Auger** *Röding 1798* (to 15cm/6in) *Indo-Pacific U.* A tall, slender shell, mature specimens having at least 20 whorls. It is pink-beige, with large white spots on the posterior part of each whorl.

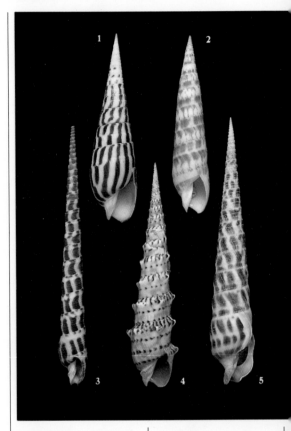

1 *TEREBRA STRIGATA* **Zebra-striped Auger** *Sowerby 1825* (10cm/4in) *W Central America* **C**. A solid, heavy shell, tapering from a wide body whorl. There are axial ridges on the early whorls and a spiral groove around each whorl. The coloration is cream, with dark-brown axial stripes.

2 *TEREBRA CHLORATA* **Chlorate Auger** *Lamarck 1822* (6cm/2¼in) *Indo-Pacific* **C**. A short, stocky species with rather convex sides, this shell is cream, with spiral rows of blue-grey squares and blotches. There are some fine axial streaks.

3 *TEREBRA COMMACULATA* **Many-spotted Auger** *Gmelin 1791* (10cm/4in) *Indo-Pacific* **U**. A tall and narrow shell with about 25 whorls. It is cream, with strong, vertical axial streaks of dark brown and fine spiral ridges.

4 *TEREBRA CRENULATA* **Crenulated Auger** *L. 1758* (10cm/4in) *Indo-Pacific* **C**. The shell is distinctly marked and sculptured and has about 16 whorls, with sharp nodules on the posterior part of each. It is beige, with spiral rows of broken dots and dashes and there are axial streaks of brown on and between the nodules.

5 *TEREBRA ROBUSTA* **Robust Auger** *Hinds 1844* (12cm/4¾in). A solid shell of moderate size with fine axial striae or growth lines. The background is cream, with large brown streaks and blotches. There are fine spiral grooves, especially on the earlier whorls.

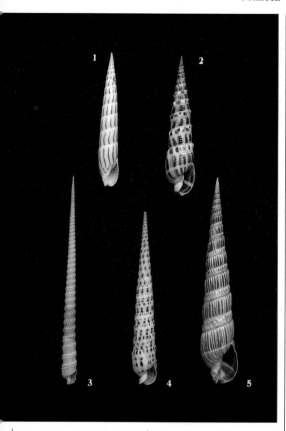

1 *TEREBRA LANCEATA* **Lance Auger** L. 1767 (4cm/1½in) *Indo-Pacific* **C**. This highly glossy, rather small slim shell has slightly convex sides and is pale cream in colour, with fine, vertical, brown axial streaks.

2 *TEREBRA VARIEGATA* **Variegated Auger** Gray 1834 (7cm/2¾in) *W Central America* **U**. A short, rather angled shell with one deep and several fine spiral grooves on brown axially streaked whorls. There are brown spiral spots between the low shoulder ribs.

3 *TEREBRA TRISERIATA* **Triseriate Auger** Gray 1834 (10cm/4in) *Japan to Philippines* **U**. A very fine, narrow shell comprising at least 40 whorls – a collectors' item. It is beige, with two rows of spiral beads on the posterior part of each whorl, between which are fine, beaded cancellations.

4 *TEREBRA CORRUGATA* **Corrugated Auger** Lamarck 1822 (10cm/4in) *W Africa* **U**. A narrow species with about 24 whorls. The shoulders bear minute pustules and the shell has axial spots and small blotches of dark brown.

5 *TEREBRA DUSSUMIERI* Kiener 1839 (8cm/3⅛in) *Japan–Taiwan* **U**. A fairly robust shell with distinctive axial ribbing. It is generally beige-brown and the anterior part of each whorl bears a spiral groove, above which there is spiral beading.

1

Turridae The Turrids are one of
the largest molluscan families,
with more than 1000 species.
Many are less than 1cm ($\frac{1}{2}$in) in
length, but all possess turret-
shaped spires and have a
characteristic notch in the
posterior part of the lip. These
species are all carnivorous and use
a dart to poison their prey.
1 *THATCHERIA MIRABILIS*
Miraculous Thatcher Shell
Angas 1877 (8cm/3$\frac{1}{4}$in) *Japan to N
Australia U.* A superbly
sculptured shell which has long
been prized by collectors. The
original specimen was purchased
in Japan by a Charles Thatcher
and, because Angas was unable to
place it in a known genus at that
time, Thatcher gained
immortality in name at least.

More shells came to light in the
1930s and the species was
assigned to the Turrids. In the
1960s and '70s many were
available in Taiwan, but this
source is now slowly
deteriorating. More recently, the
deep waters off northwestern
Australia have offered larger,
lighter specimens.

The shell has between seven
and nine whorls with angular
shoulders which are carinated.
The wide shoulder area is slightly
concave and spirals upwards
ramp-like, giving the shell its
characteristic pagoda-like
appearance. The body whorl
tapers to a wide canal and the
aperture is also wide. The interior
and columella are white, while the
rest of the shell is creamy-flesh.

1 *TURRICULA JAVANUM* **Java Turrid** *L. 1758* (6cm/2¼in) *Japan and W Pacific* **C**. A dull-brown shell with strong shoulder nodules and spiral ridges below the suture. The spire is high and the canal relatively long.

2 *COMITAS KADERLYI* **Kaderly's Turrid** *Lischke 1872* (to 10cm/4in) *Japan to NW Australia* **U**. This deepwater shell has a tall spire and a moderate canal. It is creamy white, with nodules on the whorls, but not on the body whorl, and an incised suture.

3 *COMITAS KAMAKURANA Pilsbry 1895* (5cm/2in) *Japan–Philippines* **U**. The shell is cream, with brown markings, although deep-water specimens are near-white. The spire is tall and the canal moderate and there are strongly

ridged whorls and fine spiral lirae.

4 *POLYSTIRA ALBIDA* **White Turrid** *Perry 1811* (9cm/3½in) *Caribbean* **C**. A heavy, white shell with strong spiral ridges, this species is almost always scarred.

5 *TURRIS CRISPA* **Supreme Turrid** *Lamarck 1816* (to 15cm/6in) *Indo-Pacific* **C**. A fusiform shell with a tall spire and a long canal. Variable in colour but generally white with dark axial streaks and dashes, it also has spiral ridges.

6 *GEMMULA UNEDO* **Unedo Turrid** *Kiener 1839* (10cm/4in) *Indo-Pacific* **C**. The depicted shell lives at a depth of 400m (1310ft) off NW Australia. It is a thick, heavy turrid, pale cream in colour, although occasionally orange, with fine spiral beading.

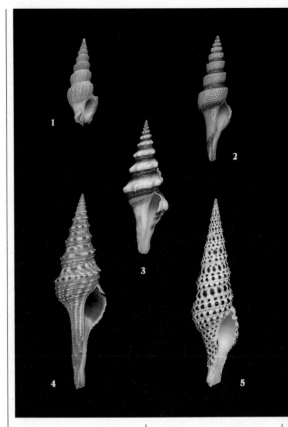

1 *DRILLIA ROSACEA* **Rose Turrid**
Reeve 1845 (3cm/1¼in) *W Africa* **U**.
Trawled in moderate depths, this
high-spired shell has fine spiral
grooves and strong axial ribs. It is
a delicate pink, with a deeper
colour to the canal area and the
inside of the lip.
2 *FUSITURRIS UNDATIRUGA*
Wrinkled Turrid *Bivona 1832*
(to 5cm/2in) *Mediterranean* **U**. An
inhabitant of medium depths,
this species has a tall spire with
vertical-sided whorls. These have
beading in oblique rows but the
moderate canal lacks it.
3 *KNEFASTIA TUBERCULIFERA*
Knobbed Turrid *Broderip and
Sowerby 1829* (6cm/2¼in) *W
Central America* **U**. This shell has
a tall spire and a moderate canal
and the broad shoulders bear

blunt nodules. It has alternating
brown and white bands, with
pale-orange coloration on the
nodules and the body whorl.
4 *LOPHIOTOMA INDICA* **Indian
Turrid** *Röding 1798* (9cm/3½in) *S
India to Australia* **C**. A dweller in
moderately deep water, with a
tall spire and a long canal. It has
concave whorls with sharp
shoulders and spiral ridges
bearing brown-white dashes.
There are brown axial streaks.
5 *TURRIS BABYLONIA* **Babylonia
Turrid** *L. 1758* (9cm/3½in) *W
Pacific* **U**. An inhabitant of
shallow to deep water, with a tall
spire and a moderate canal. There
are coarse spiral ridges covered
with black dots or blotches of
varying size. The shell
occasionally has yellow bands.

Acteonidae A small group of medium-sized shells which are mostly ovate to fusiform. Some species are highly patterned.

1 *ACTEON ELOISAE* **Eloise's Acteon** *Abbott 1973* (to 3cm/1¼in) *Oman U.* An ovate shell with a low spire, this collectors' favourite is an intertidal species. It has spiral grooves and is basically off-white, with vivid tan blotches ringed in black.

Hydatinidae Bubble shells are thin and quite colourful and some species are very fragile. They live in sand in warm seas.

2 *HYDATINA PHYSIS* **Paper Bubble** *L. 1758* (5cm/2in) *Indo-Pacific C.* A delicate, thin, and rounded shell with a depressed spire. It has fine dark lines on a pale olive-green background.

3 *HYDATINA ALBOCINCTA* **White-banded Bubble** *Van der Hoeven 1839* (4cm/1½in) *Taiwan C.* This thin and fragile species has a depressed spire and there are broad alternating spiral bands of brown and cream.

4 *HYDATINA ZONATA* **Zoned Bubble** *Lightfoot 1786* (4cm/1½in) *Indo-Pacific U.* An inhabitant of shallow water to 50m (165ft), this shell is globose, with a sunken spire. It is off-white and has fine growth lines. There are four brown spiral bands.

5 *AMPLUSTRUM AMPLUSTRE* **Amplustre Bubble** *L. 1758* (2.5cm/1in) *Indo-Pacific C.* This small, pretty shell is thin and light and has a flat spire. It is pale pink, with three broad, spiral bands.

Arcacea

Arcidae These shells are generally ovate to oblong, with a long, straight hinge on which there are many fine, interlocking teeth. They usually live anchored to rocks and other substrates by a byssus of hair. Most species are edible.

1 *TRISIDOS SEMITORTA* **Half-propellor Ark** *Lamarck 1819* (10cm/4in) *Japan to Philippines C.* This large and rather heavy shell is twisted posteriorly and the umbones are off-centre. It has a long, straight hinge line with toxodont teeth. The interior is yellow and the exterior white, with concentric growth lines and fine radial ribs. The species is a shallow-water dweller.

2 *ANADARA MACULOSA* **Maculose Ark** *Reeve 1844* (10cm/4in) *SW Pacific C.* A thick and heavy shell, white throughout. There are strong radial ribs and a few concentric growth lines.

Limopsacea

Glycymeridae These shells are solid, rather rounded, and equivalved. They have a porcellaneous interior and a thick periostracum.

3 *GLYCYMERIS GIGANTEA* **Giant Bittersweet** *Reeve 1843* (to 10cm/4in) *W Central America C.* A shallow-water species with thick, heavy valves and central umbones. The shell has fine concentric and radial lirae and is white-beige, with vivid brown streaks. There are coarse, shallow teeth.

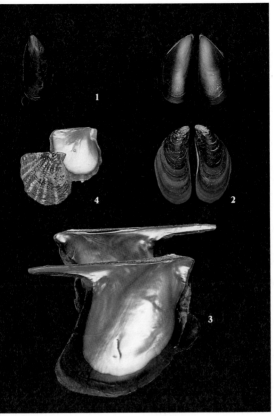

Mytilacea

Mytilidae Mussels occur worldwide, mainly in shallow, intertidal water. They have a few small teeth and a weak hinge. These species usually live attached to rocks, where they form colonies. Many species of mussel are edible.

1 *MYTILUS EDULIS* **Common Blue Mussel** L. *1758* (7cm/2¾in) *Worldwide (except for polar seas)* **A**. A rather elongate and pointed species, with sharp umbones, this dweller on intertidal rocks has been a seafood since early times.

2 *PERNA VIRIDIS* **Green Mussel** L. *1758* (7cm/2¾in) *SW Pacific* **C**. This shallow-water dweller has a black-green periostracum and an iridescent cream interior. There is a small tooth in the right valve.

Pteriacea

Pteriidae Wing and Pearl Oysters are a large, mainly tropical, family. They have highly nacreous interiors and some produce pearls.

3 *PTERIA PENGUIN* **Penguin Wing Oyster** *Röding 1798* (to 20cm/8in) *Indo-Pacific* **C**. A black, ovate shallow-water dweller with a hinge which is elongated posteriorly and extends into a sharp, narrow projection. The interior is nacreous.

4 *PINCTADA MARGARITIFERA* **Black-lipped Pearl Oyster** L. *1758* (to 20cm/8in) *Indo-Pacific* **C**. This shell has solid, rather compressed valves and a black-edged nacreous interior. It is used widely in shellcraft.

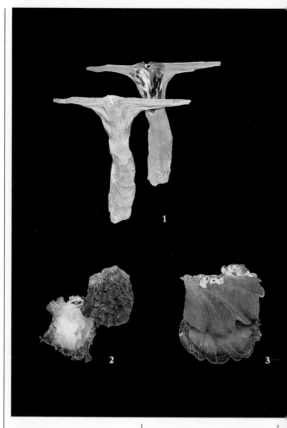

Malleidae The Hammer
Oysters, so-called because some
species are hammer-shaped, have
semi-nacreous interiors. Most
species are tropical and live in
association with corals.
1 *MALLEUS ALBUS* **White
Hammer Oyster** *Lamarck 1819*
(16cm/6¼in) *Indo-Pacific C.* This
species lives on grass and rocks in
shallow water. It has a hinge line
which is elongated both
posteriorly and anteriorly. The
body is rather irregular, oblong,
and rough, with a cream
coloration, and the nacreous
interior is small and pale-blue-
white.

Ostreacea
Ostreidae These, the true
oysters, occur worldwide and are

a major source of food. Most are
of a dull appearance but there is
considerable variation in form.
2 *OSTREA IMBRICATA* **Imbricate
Oyster** *Lamarck 1819* (to 10cm/
4in) *Japan C.* This shallow-water
dweller is roughly ovate, very
scaly, and has imbricate valves of
a dark purple. The interior is
white and semi-nacreous. The
ligament is short.
3 *LOPHA CRISTAGALLI* **Cock's-
comb Oyster** *L. 1758* (10cm/4in)
Indo-Pacific C. A deep-purple
shallow-water dweller, this shell
has a few sharp radial ribs with
deeply incised hollows which
reveal a zigzag central margin. It
grows spines with which it clasps
corals and other substrates.

Pectinidae Scallops form a substantial family and are both popular with collectors and an important food source. They occur worldwide and are highly mobile, moving rather like butterflies by flapping open and shut both shell valves. There is a great variation in colour and pattern, but the overall shape remains fairly uniform.

1 *AEQUIPECTEN OPERCULARIS* **Queen Scallop** L. *1758* (7cm/ 2¾in) *NE Atlantic and Mediterranean **C**.* This food source is variable in colour, being pink, yellow, mauve, or brown. It has rounded valves with flattish radial ribs. There are fine radial striae and the ears are almost equal.

2 *PECTEN MAXIMUS JACOBAEUS*

St James's Scallop L. *1758* (12cm/4¾in) *Mediterranean and NW Africa **C**.* An edible scallop similar in shape to *Pecten maximus* but smaller and with ribs which are more angular and ridged. The right valve is usually white, while the ribs on the left valve are sometimes mottled with brown-pink.

3 *PECTEN MAXIMUS* **Great Scallop** L. *1758* (to 15cm/6in) *NE Atlantic **C**.* This major source of seafood inhabits both shallow and deep water. The valves are unequal but the ears are equal. The right valve is concave, the left convex to flat. The shell has strong radial, flat ribs. It is creamy, with, occasionally, a mottled brown-pink coloration on the umbo areas.

1 *AMUSIUM LAURENTI* **Laurent's Moon Scallop** *Gmelin 1791* (7cm/2¾in) *Caribbean U*. This shell, which lives at depths of 50–200m (165–655ft), has rounded, smooth valves with even ears. Both valves are convex and one is brown with dark radial rays, the other pure white. The interior is white, with fine radial ribs towards the ventral margin.

2 *AMUSIUM BALLOTI* **Ballot's Moon Scallop** *Bernardi 1861* (to 13cm/5in) *N Australia U*. The valves are rounded and very shiny, the ears low and even. One valve is orange-brown with concentric growth lines, the other white. The interior is white, with fine radial ribs.

3 *PROTEOPECTEN GLABER* **Bald Scallop** *L. 1758* (4cm/1½in) *Mediterranean C*. This species occurs at depths down to 900m (2650ft). Its coloration and patterning vary considerably, the shell being found in almost every shade from albino to almost black. Both valves are rather convex and the ears are almost even. There are nine or ten radial folds.

4 *CHLAMYS ISLANDICA* **Iceland Scallop** *Müller 1776* (8cm/3¼in) *Arctic Sea and Atlantic C*. An inhabitant of moderate depths, this shell has convex, rounded valves and a larger anterior ear. The interior is whitish. There are rough radial ridges and the shell's coloration ranges from beige, through pink, to deep-brown-purple.

1 *GLORIPALLIUM PALLIUM*
Mantle Scallop *L. 1758* (to 8cm/
3¼in) *Indo-Pacific **C***. An
attractive, colourful, shallow-reef
dweller, this shell has rounded,
equal valves and uneven ears. It is
radially ribbed, with grooves and
fine concentric scales. The left
valve is slightly more colourful,
with yellow-orange ribs and vivid
concentric streaks or larger
patches of orange to crimson.
2 *SWIFTOPECTEN SWIFTI* **Swift's
Scallop** *Bernardi 1858* (to 12cm/
4¾in) *Japan **C***. A thick, heavy,
shallow-water shell with fan-
shaped valves, the left one of
which is deep-pink-white, with
five radial folds bearing low,
rounded knobs. The concentric
growth stages are clearly
noticeable. The right valve is

usually pale-pink-white. The ears
are uneven.
3 *CHLAMYS NOBILIS* **Noble
Scallop** *Reeve 1852* (to 10cm/4in)
*Japan to Philippines **C***. Occurring
in bright pink, yellow, orange,
red, and purple, this shallow-
water shell is a collectors'
favourite. The valves are equal
and rounded, the ears almost
equal. There are at least 20 finely
striated radial ribs.
4 *CHLAMYS SENATORIA* **Senate
Scallop** *Gmelin 1791* (to 7cm/
2¾in) *Indo-Pacific **C***. An offshore
species with fan-shaped, equal
valves and uneven ears. There is
radial ridging and the shell has a
byssal notch. The species exhibits
an almost infinite array of colours
arranged in mottled, irregular
patches on both valves.

1 *EQUICHLAMYS BIFRONS*
Bifron's Scallop *Lamarck 1819*
(8cm/3¼in) *S Australia* **C**. This
shallow-water species has
rounded and rather flat equal
valves and even ears. The left
valve is pastel mauve, with about
eight darker-coloured, low radial
ribs. The interior is deep magenta.
2 *MESOPEPLUM CONVEXUM*
Grooved Fan Shell *Quoy and
Gaimard 1835* (5cm/2in) *New
Zealand* **U**. Usually caught in nets
or dredged in deep water, this
species has uneven ears and
convex valves which have
undulating radial ribbing with
fine secondary grooves. The
colour ranges from pink to red,
and occasionally purple.
3 *CHLAMYS LUCULENTA* **White-
streaked Scallop** *Reeve 1853*

(4cm/1½in) *Philippines and N
Australia* **C**. The valves are very
flat and equal, the ears uneven.
There is a distinct byssal notch
and the shell has fine, scaly radial
riblets. The colour variation is
vast, embracing red, yellow,
orange and brown, among other
colours. There are very fine
concentric and irregular white
lines below the umbo area.
4 *CHLAMYS AUSTRALIS* **Austral
Scallop** *Sowerby 1847* (to 10cm/
4in) *S and W Australia* **C**. The
shell is similar in appearance to
Chlamys nobilis, but its valves are
more rounded and convex. The
radial ribs have fine scales or
minute spines which have a rough
texture. This offshore species
exhibits a wide variation in
colour.

1 *LYROPECTEN NODOSA* **Lion's Paw** L. *1758* (to 11cm/4¼in) *Caribbean* **U**. A prized collectors' item, this species is thick and coarsely sculptured, with about eight prominent, rounded ribs on which, in adult shells, there are high, rounded nodules. There are radial grooves between the ribs. The shell, which lives at depths of 10–50m (35–165ft), is usually dull-red-brown.

2 *PECTEN ZICZAC* **Zigzag Scallop** L. *1758* (8cm/3⅛in) *Caribbean* **U**. A rounded, smooth, and glossy shell with uneven valves and even ears. There are about 25 radial grooves and concentric growth lines on the deeply convex right or upper valve and the slightly concave left valve has closer radial grooves. The umbones are red, brown, and white. The shell lives at depths of 1–6om (3–195ft).

3 *ARGOPECTEN CIRCULARIS* **Circular Scallop** *Sowerby 1835* (to 10cm/4in) *W Central America* **C**. This edible shell lives at depths to 100m (330ft) and has rounded, equal, inflated, and convex valves. Its ears are even and the radial ribs are low. The shell is basically white, with irregular mottled and radial stripes and patches of yellow, orange, or purple. Other colorations occur, ranging almost to black.

4 *ARGOPECTEN GIBBUS* **Calico Scallop** L. *1758* (6cm/2⅜in) *Caribbean* **C**. This shell is rather similar to *Argopecten circularis*, but its even ears are somewhat lower and less extended. The species is edible.

1 *GLORIPALLIUM SANGUINOLENTA* **Blood-stained Scallop** *Gmelin 1791* (to 5cm/2in) *Red Sea* **R**. An inhabitant of shallow coral reefs, this shell has sturdy, fan-shaped, deep, flattish valves and uneven ears. There are about nine pink-blotched ribs with fine, concentric lamellae which are rough to the touch. The interior has purple margins.

2 *PECTEN IMBRICATA* **Little Knobbly Scallop** *Gmelin 1791* (to 4cm/1½in) *Caribbean* **U**. This shell, which lives at depths down to 20m (65ft), is rounded, with uneven ears, the anterior one of which is sharply elongated. There are strong, hollow nodules on the seven or so radial ribs. The shell is pink and white, with a yellow interior.

3 *DECATOPECTEN LANGFORDI* **Langford's Scallop** *Dall, Bartsch, and Rehder 1938* (5cm/2in) *Central Pacific* **R**. An offshore species found at depths down to 100m (333ft), this shell has valves which are small, rounded, and deeply convex. There are concentric markings of yellow, orange, and pink, and the interior is pink, yellow, and white. The radial ribs are slightly nodulose.

4 *ANGUIPECTEN SUPERBUS* **Superb Scallop** *Sowerby 1842* (7cm/2¾in) *Japan to Philippines* **U**. Found in shallow water to a depth of 8om (26ft), this species is fan-shaped, with very narrow dorsal margins and ears. There is radial ribbing. The exterior has irregular pink-orange blotches and the interior is white.

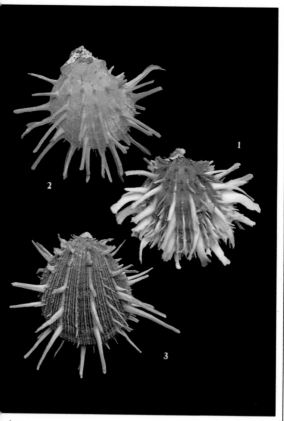

Spondylidae Thorny Oysters or, more aptly, Chrysanthemum Shells, live attached permanently to corals and rocks. All possess a characteristic "ball-and-socket" hinge. Variation in form and colour can hinder identification.
1 *SPONDYLUS PRINCEPS* **Pacific Thorny Oyster** *Broderip 1833* (to 13cm/5in) *W Central America C.* The valves in this offshore species are equal and convex and have flattish radial ribs from which extend many short to medium-length (3cm/1¾) spines, most of which are spatulate. The right valve is usually more spinose.
2 *SPONDYLUS AMERICANUS* **American Thorny Oyster** *Hermann 1781* (to 20cm/8in) *Caribbean C.* A large, showy shell

in which the valves are rounded and convex, with even ears. Choice specimens are much prized. There are low radial ribs from which grow very long (up to 5cm/2in) rounded or flattened spines. The right valve is usually more spinose. The species lives on rocks and wrecks at depths down to 50m (165ft).
3 *SPONDYLUS REGIUS* **Regal Thorny Oyster** *L. 1758* (to 20cm/8in) *W Pacific C.* A large and impressive shell with equal, very convex valves. It has coarse radial ribs and ridges with both very long and short sharp spines. The two valves are equally spinose. The coloration is vivid orange to dull pink. This shell lives on rocks at depths of 5–50m (15–65ft).

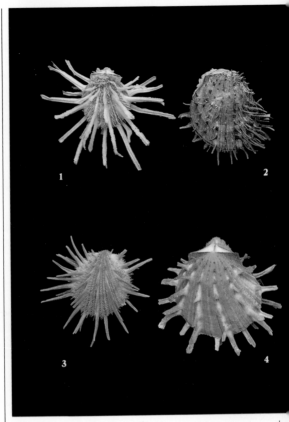

1 *SPONDYLUS WRIGHTIANUS*
Wright's Thorny Oyster *Crosse*
1872 (to 15cm/6in) *W Australia* **C**.
A pretty, delicate, deep-water
species with flattish, equal valves
and even ears. There are many
spinose ribs and the spines are
often long and flat. The coloration
is white to lavender, with orange-
mauve umbones and the inner
margins are crenulated.
2 *SPONDYLUS GAEDEROPUS L.*
1758 (to 10cm/4in) *Mediterranean*
C. This thick shell lives in
intertidal and shallow water and
has unequal valves. The right is
convex with ribs and concentric
lamellae bearing spines. This
valve is brown to mauve-red,
while the left is usually whitish,
with tinted spines.
3 *SPONDYLUS IMPERIALIS*

Imperial Thorny Oyster
Chenu 1843 (12cm/4¾in) *Japan to*
Philippines **C**. This ovate shell
lives in water ranging from
shallow to deep. It has equal
valves, and there are about six
main ribs, with long, mainly
straight spines between which are
many fine ribs bearing short,
sharp spines. The shell is basically
white, with pinkish tints.
4 *SPONDYLUS SINENSIS Schreibers*
1793 (to 10cm/4in) *SW Pacific* **C**.
A smallish, heavy, coral-dwelling
shell with convex, equal valves.
There are five or six low ribs from
which grow relatively few short-
to-medium length, sometimes
spatulate, spines. The shell is
beige-brown, but deep-orange-red
at the umbones.

1 *SPONDYLUS SQUAMOSUS*
Brown-striped Thorny Oyster *Schreibers 1793* (8cm/3¼in) *SW Pacific* **C**. An inhabitant of dead corals and wrecks, irregularly ovate to rounded, with broad, depressed ribs bearing short, sometimes curved, white, spatulate spines. The umbones are irregular and red-brown.

2 *SPONDYLUS VARIANS* **The Water Thorny Oyster** *Sowerby 1829* (to 20cm/8in) *Philippines* **U**. An ovate, solid, and heavy shell which lives on dead corals and wrecks. It is pure white and covered with many short, sharp spines, those near the margin being longer. The umbonal area is highly coloured, and is usually red-orange. The upper valve is flattish, the lower concave. Inside both valves are large depressions which are usually filled with sea water and covered with a thin, calcareous membrane. There is a large attachment area.

Anomiacea
Anomiidae Mostly thin and semi-translucent, these shells are plentiful in shallow waters. They attach themselves to rocks and to marine debris.

3 *PLACUNA PLACENTA* **Window-pane Oyster** *L. 1758* (to 15cm/6in) *Central Philippines* **A**. A round, flat, and semi-transparent species with very fine, concentric ornamentation. It is found in shallow water. The interior is nacreous, shiny, and clear, and has inverted V-shaped teeth. The species is used in shellcraft.

1
2
3
4

Trigoniacea

Trigoniidae The Brooch Clams were a large group in early geological times, but few species now exist.

1 *NEOTRIGONIA BEDNALLI*
Bednall's Brooch Clam *Verco 1907* (3cm/1¼in) *SE Australia* **C**.
This species is dredged offshore. It has dark-brown strong, scaly, radial ridges and the nacreous interior is lavender or yellow.

Limacea

Limidae File Clams have rough, file-like surfaces and are highly mobile, swimming with the help of long tentacles.

2 *LIMA LIMA* **Rough File Clam**
L. 1758 (to 10cm/4in) *Caribbean and W Pacific* **C**. This shell has equal valves and a long-sided

anterior slope. It is off-white and there are many radial, rounded, lamellate ribs. The specimen shown is the larger form, *Lima vulgaris*, Link 1807.

Lucinacea

Lucinidae A large family of mainly white and circular shells, distributed worldwide.

3 *FIMBRIA SOVERBII* **Elegant Fimbria** *Reeve 1841* (10cm/4in)
SW Pacific **R**. A thick, heavy, ovate shell, this shallow-water dweller has concentric, raised, dentate and anteriorly lamellose narrow ridges.

4 *CODAKIA TIGERINA* **Pacific Tiger Lucine** *L. 1758* (to 10cm/ 4in) *Indo-Pacific* **C**. A rounded, thick shell with fine radial and concentric reticulation.

Chamacea
Chamidae A smallish family,
these species are known as Jewel
Boxes and live attached to rocks
and wrecks. They have crude
teeth and most are colourful.
1 CHAMA BRASSICA **Cabbage
Jewel Box** Reeve 1846 (6cm/2¼in)
Philippines U. A heavy and thick
species with concentric rows of
foliated lamellae and anchorage
debris on the left valve.
2 CHAMA LAZARUS **Lazarus
Jewel Box** L. 1758 (10cm/4in)
Indo-Pacific C. This shallow-
water dweller has numerous flat
and scaly lamellae, some of which
extend into forked spines. The left
valve bears attachment debris
and is very irregular.
3 ECHINOCHAMA BRASILIANA
Spiny Jewel Box Nicol 1953

(5cm/2in) Brazil C. An inhabitant
of rocks in shallow water, this
pinkish-beige shell is ovate and
has curved umbones. A rounded
lunule is present and the radial
ribs are highly spinose.

Carditacea
Carditidae Most of these shells
are found in shallow tropical
waters. They are thick and solid,
with predominantly radial ribs.
4 CARDITA CRASSICOSTATA **Rosy
Cardita** Lamarck 1819 (5cm/2in)
Sulu Sea–Australia C. An
elongate shell with large, hollow,
scaly ribs, this species lives in
fairly shallow water to a depth of
100m (330ft). Its coloration varies
from pink to yellow or red-brown
and the interior is white. It is
often lime- or coral-encrusted.

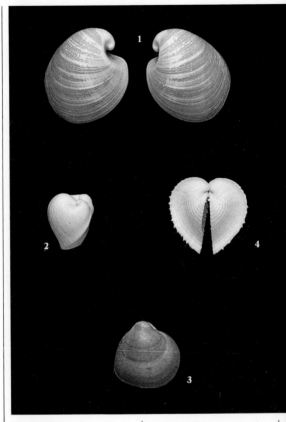

Glossacea

Glossidae Heart Clams are an ancient group with few modern survivors. The umbones are coiled and, with inflated shells, give the characteristic heart shape.

1 *GLOSSUS HUMANUS* **Ox Heart** *L. 1758* (9cm/3½in) *NE Atlantic and Mediterranean C.* The species lives in water ranging from shallow to very deep. It is rounded and inflated, with rolled umbones coiled anteriorly.

2 *ISOCARDIA MOLTKIANA* **Moltke's Heart Clam** *Spengler 1783* (4cm/1½in) *SW Pacific U.* This shallow-water species has a keeled dorsal margin, concentric grooves, and tightly curved umbones.

Cardiacea

Cardiidae Cockles are a large and well-known family in which there is great variation in shape and colour. They are very active, moving about by means of a long and powerful foot.

3 *NEMOCARDIUM BECHEI* **De la Beche's Cockle** *Reeve 1847* (6cm/2½in) *Japan to Australia U.* Found at moderate depths, this shell has very fine radial and concentric striae, and at the posterior end there are pronounced radial, slightly spinose, ridges.

4 *CORCULUM CARDISSA* **True Heart Cockle** *L. 1758* (to 5cm/2in) *Indo-Pacific C.* A heart-shaped shell with a thin, lateral keel. The surfaces are convex and there are concentric ridges.

1 *CTENOCARDIA VICTOR* **Victor Cockle** *Angas 1872* (4cm/1½in) *W Pacific* **U**. An ovate shell with inflated umbones, this is a collectors' favourite. There is an angular ridge from the umbones to the ventral margin. The radial ribs have sharp, short, curved spines. The shell lives at depths to 100m (330ft).

2 *FRAGUM UNEDO* **Unedo Cockle** *L. 1758* (5cm/2in) *Indo-Pacific* **C**. A thick, heavy, and roughly quadrangular shell with an angular ridge from the umbones to the ventral margin. There are many low ribs with irregular, crimson, concentric scales.

3 *TRACHYCARDIUM MAGNUM* **Magnum Cockle** *L. 1758* (9cm/3½in) *Caribbean* **U**. An ovate and elongate shallow-water dweller with narrow umbones and strong and rounded ribs which are minutely nodulose at the posterior end.

4 *CERASTODERMA EDULE* **Common European Cockle** *L. 1758* (5cm/2in) *NE Atlantic* **A**. This well-known seafood shell is farmed commercially. It is trigonal and thick, with scaly radial ribs, concentric growth lines, and small teeth.

5 *ACANTHOCARDIA TUBERCULATA* **Tuberculate Cockle** *L. 1758* (6cm/2½in) *NE Atlantic and Mediterranean* **C**. A thick and heavy shell with rounded and convex valves, this species lives in shallow water to a depth of 100m (330ft). It has strong radial ribs and concentric growth lines.

1

2

3

4

1 *CARDIUM COSTATUM* **Costate Cockle** *L. 1758* (10cm/4in) *W Africa C.* This prized collectors' shell is relatively thin but strong and has high, hollow, keeled ribs. There are very fine concentric striae on the interstices and the valves gape at the posterior end. This shallow-water shell is off-white and occasionally has broad orange-brown streaks.

2 *ACANTHOCARDIA ECHINATA* **Prickly Cockle** *L. 1758* (7cm/ 2¾in) *NE Atlantic and Mediterranean C.* A shallow-water dweller of medium size, this shell is broadly oval with low radial ribs which have strong, rounded spines or sharp tubercules. The umbones and the area immediately below them are relatively smooth. The shell is

cream-white and has a white interior.

3 *LAEVICARDIUM ELATUM* **Giant Pacific Egg Cockle** *Sowerby 1833* (15cm/6in) *W Central America C.* A large and inflated species with many fine, flat ribs and a smooth umbo. There are concentric growth lines. The posterior side and lunule area are smooth. The exterior is yellow, the interior cream.

4 *PLAGIOCARDIUM PSEUDOLIMA* **Giant Cockle** *Lamarck 1819* (15cm/6in) *E Africa C.* Probably the largest species in the family, this shell is rounded, thick, and heavy. It has inflated and rounded umbones and squarish radial ribs with small, scaly spines near the margins. It is a subtidal dweller.

1

Tridacnidae A small group of large and very large, heavy shells, some with attractive ornamentation. They inhabit coral reefs, mainly in tropical areas of the Indo-Pacific region.
1 *TRIDACNA GIGAS* **Giant Clam** *L. 1758* (to 1.2m/4ft) *SW Pacific* *U*. The legendary Giant Clam is a truly unique shell. By far the largest and heaviest of all molluscs, it exceeds 1m (3¼ft) in width and can weigh over 200 kilograms. Contrary to widespread belief, it is not a maneater but feeds on the marine algae which grow within its fleshy mantle. The species can produce a porcellaneous, non-precious pearl which in some cases reaches the size of a golf ball.

The shell lives with its hinge side downwards, embedded in coral or rock. This position allows sunlight to reach the large, fleshy blue, green, or yellowish mantle which envelops the large, gaping aperture. The outer shell itself bears four or five undulating radial ribs which are generally completely encrusted with lime and coral debris and other marine growth. The shell is dull-grey-cream in colour.

Large, heavy specimens are usually fished from shallow depths by means of a strong chain and pulley used from an anchored fishing boat. Overcollecting has led to this species being protected by local fishing restrictions and international permits are required for its collection.

1 *TRIDACNA SQUAMOSA* **Fluted Clam** *Lamarck 1819* (to 25cm/10in) *Indo-Pacific C.* A medium-sized, heavy shell, this species is trigonal and has broad, rounded radial ribs bearing hollow scales or flutes. There is a lateral byssal gape. An inhabitant of coral reefs, the shell is cream, yellow, pink, or orange, with a white interior.

2 *TRIDACNA MAXIMA* **Elongated Clam** *Röding 1798* (20cm/8in) *Indo-Pacific C.* A rather elongated shell, with undulating folds and low, hollow lamellar scales. It has a large byssal gape behind the umbones. Found on coral reefs, it is cream-white and occasionally has yellow or orange bands.

3 *HIPPOPUS HIPPOPUS* **Bear's Paw Clam** *L. 1758* (20cm/8in)

SW Pacific C. A large, heavy, trigonal shell with very inflated valves which have irregular radial folds and riblets, some bearing small prickly spines ventrally. There is a flat-ribbed lunule depression below the raised and incurved umbones. This dweller in shallow reefs is cream, with crimson concentric blotches and yellow tints at the margins.

4 *HIPPOPUS PORCELLANUS* **China Clam** *Rosewater 1982* (20cm/8in) *S Philippines C.* Similar to *Hippopus hippopus*, but with more rounded margins and a proportionately lighter, thinner shell, this species is found on coral reefs. The shell is an overall cream, but the umbones are mottled with yellow and pink and the interior is white.

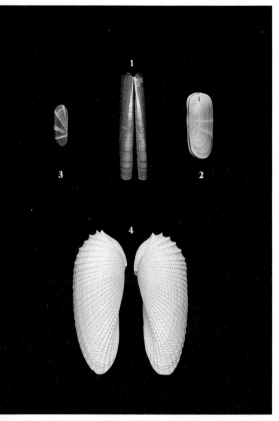

Solenacea
Solenidae Razor shells are well-known shallow-water burrowers, many possessing long, slender shells. They are distributed worldwide.
1 *ENSIS SILIQUA* **Giant Razor Shell** *L. 1758* (to 20cm/8in) *NE Atlantic* **C**. This long, straight, and narrow sand-dweller has gaping valves and, posteriorly, a hinge and a tiny tooth.
2 *SOLECURTUS STRIGILATUS* **Scraper Clam** *L. 1758* (8cm/3¼in) *Mediterranean and NW Africa* **C**. An inhabitant of intertidal mud flats, this species has convex, gaping valves with fine, concentric growth striae and oblique, wavy grooves.
3 *SILIQUA RADIATA* **Sunset Siliqua** *L. 1758* (8cm/3¼in) *Indian Ocean* **C**. A very thin, light, elongate, and ovate shell with a tiny hinge near the anterior end.

Pholadacea
Pholadidae Distributed worldwide, the Piddocks are bivalves capable of boring into mud, clay, wood, and even rock.
4 *CYRTOPLEURA COSTATA* **Angel's Wings** *L. 1758* (15cm/6in) *Florida and Caribbean* **C**. The largest member of the family, this shell has valves which are elongate and convex, particularly at the umbones, and it gapes at both ends. The strong radial ribs are lamellose and rough to the touch. There is a spoon-shaped process in each valve and the interior is smooth and white. The species lives in deep mud.

Tellinidae These thin, rather oval shells are distributed more or less worldwide and there are many colourful tropical species in the family. All Tellins possess small cardinal teeth.

1 *PHYLLODA FOLIACEA* **Foliated Tellin** *L. 1758* (7cm/2¾in) *Gulf of Oman and Indo-Pacific C.* A bright-orange shallow-water dweller with flat, equal valves and a keel from the umbones to the lower posterior margins. The ligament line is uneven and slightly spinose.

2 *TELLINA RADIATA* **Sunrise Tellin** *L. 1758* (7cm/2¾in) *Caribbean C.* An elongate, smooth, and glossy shell which lives in coral sand in shallow water. There are small cardinal teeth.

3 *TELLINA VIRGATA* **Virgate Tellin** *L. 1758* (7cm/2¾in) *Indo-Pacific C.* This shallow-water species is ovate, with a matt, concentrically grooved surface and a deep groove from the umbo to the posterior margin.

Donacidae This family is distributed worldwide and comprises mostly small, wedge-shaped shells, some of which are brightly coloured.

4 *DONAX SERRA* **Giant South African Wedge** *Röding 1798* (6cm/2¼in) *South Africa C.* This thick, ovate, and elongate species is pale lilac, with a purple interior and has a cardinal tooth. The posterior area from the umbo to the margin is concentrically ridged.

Arcticacea
Arcticidae A small group of hard-shell clams similar to the Venus Clams, but with variations in the teeth.

1 *ARCTICA ISLANDICA* **Ocean Quahog** *L. 1767* (10cm/4in) *N Atlantic and North Sea* **A**. This important seafood source is thick, beige-pink, and covered with an almost black periostracum. The interior is white, with coarse cardinal teeth. The shell lives on mud in shallow water.

Veneracea
Veneridae A large and varied family of over 400 species worldwide. Cold seas provide the habitat for many edible Venus Clams, while the tropical species are colourful. All have hinges and both lateral and cardinal teeth.

2 *CALLANAITIS DISJECTA* **Wedding Cake Venus** *Perry 1811* (6cm/2¼in) *S Australia* **C**. The shell is ovate and trigonal, with a distinctive concentric ornamentation of flat, continuous frills, and the valves are convex.

3 *CIRCOMPHALUS FOLIACEOLAMELLOSUS* **Scaly Ridged Venus** *Schröter 1788* (7cm/2¾in) *W Africa* **C**. This beige-pink species is similar to *Callanaitis disjecta*, but is flatter, more solid, and has twice as many concentric lamellae.

4 *PERIGLYPTA RETICULATA* **Reticulated Venus** *L. 1758* (9cm/3½in) *Indo-Pacific* **C**. A dweller in sand in shallow water, this shell is thick and heavy and is heavily sculptured.

1 *LIOCONCHA CASTRENSIS*
Chocolate Flamed Venus L.
1758 (5cm/2in) *Indo-Pacific C.* An
inhabitant of sand in shallow
water, this species is thick and
heavy and its surface is smooth
and glossy, with very fine
concentric lirae.

2 *PAPHIA ALAPAPILIONIS*
Butterfly Venus Röding *1798*
(7cm/2¾in) *Indian Ocean C.* This
thick, glossy shell has concentric
grooves and a cream-orange
coloration, with broken brown
radial bands and a white interior.
There are small, neat cardinal
teeth.

3 *PERIGLYPTA PUERPERA*
Youthful Venus L. *1771* (9cm/
3½in) *Indo-Pacific C.* A thick, solid
shell with fine concentric and
radial striae, this species lives in

shallow water. It is off-white,
with chocolate-brown radial
bands. The interior is white, with
a purple area around the pallial
sinus.

4 *CALLISTA ERYCINA* **Red
Callista** L. *1758* (8cm/3¼in) *S
India and SW Pacific C.* This
shallow-water dweller is solid,
highly glossy, and has flat,
concentric ridges. It is cream,
with orange at the margins and
radial rays of red-brown
extending from the umbones. The
interior is white.

5 *TAPES LITTERATA* **Lettered
Venus** L. *1758* (9cm/3½in) *Indo-
Pacific C.* An ovate, trigonal shell
with rather flat valves, this
species is fairly smooth and has
very fine concentric grooves.

1 *CHIONE GNIDIA* **Gnidia Venus**
Broderip and Sowerby 1829 (to
10cm/4in) *W Central America* **C**.
In this species, the most ornate of
the family, the ovate, trigonal
valves are fawn or off-white and
matt. There are fine radial
striations and concentric lamellae
rising into prickly scales. It lives
in shallow water to a depth of
50m (165ft).
2 *MACROCALLISTA MACULATA*
Calico Clam L. *1758* (5cm/2in)
Caribbean **C**. An ovate, trigonal,
thick, and glossy shell, found in
shallow water. The background is
beige-grey, with rays of broken
pale tan in squares and blotches.
The lunule is brown.
3 *CHIONE PAPHIA* **King Venus** L.
1767 (4cm/1½in) *Caribbean* **C**. A
trigonal, thick, and rather convex

shallow-water shell with strong,
rounded, concentric ridges which
are lamellose towards the
posterior margin.
4 *DOSINIA VARIEGATA*
Variegated Dosinia *Gray 1838*
(5cm/2in) *Indo-Pacific* **C**. A
shallow-water species, rounded
and with close, coarse, narrow,
concentric ridges. There is a tiny
lunule.
5 *PITAR DIONE* **Royal Comb
Venus** L. *1758* (5cm/2in)
Caribbean **U**. Rather difficult to
obtain in recent years, this
subtidal species is triangular and
has strong, concentric ribs. There
are extended spines running
posteriorly from the umbones
towards the junction of the
posterior and ventral margins.

Myidae The Soft-shell Clams are sand or mud dwellers and most have an ovate, rough, dull shell and a brown periostracum.
1 *MYA ARENARIA* **Soft-shell Clam** *L. 1758* (9cm/3½in) *E USA and NE Atlantic* **C.** An elongate and ovate rough shell with concentric growth lines. The gaping extremities are creamy white. This species, which lives in sand or mud in shallow water, is a major seafood source.
2 *MACROCALLISTA NIMBOSA* **Sunray Venus** *Lightfoot 1786* (12cm/4¾in) *Caribbean and Florida* **C.** A large, elongate, ovate species, smooth and shiny. This shallow-water dweller is pale grey, with radial rays of darker grey and concentric growth lines.
3 *CALLISTA CHIONE* **Smooth**

Venus *L. 1758* (7cm/2¾in) *Mediterranean and NE Atlantic* **C.** This highly popular seafood lives in shallow water and to a depth of 100m (330ft). It is solid, trigonal, and glossy.
4 *PERIGLYPTA CHEMNITZI* **Chemnitz's Venus** *Hanley 1844* (10cm/4in) *SW Pacific* **C.** The convex, inflated valves are coarsely sculptured with many concentric, reticulated ridges. It is a shallow-water species.
5 *MERCENARIA MERCENARIA* **Northern Quahog** *L. 1758* (9cm/3½in) *E North America* **C.** A solid, thick shell, dull-fawn-orange in colour and with concentric growth lines. It inhabits lagoons and is a popular seafood in the USA and Europe.

Nautilidae This is the only group of cephalopods with true external shells. They are discoidal in shape and possess large apertures. Perhaps four or five species are confined to the Western Pacific, where they live in deep water. They are carnivorous and the sexes are distinct.

1 *NAUTILUS POMPILIUS*
Chambered Nautilus *L. 1758* (15cm/6in) *W Pacific **C***. Well represented in early geological times, this species is remarkable in being one of the very few in the group to survive. It is not, as once thought, a primitive shell, but is highly sophisticated and well adapted to its lifestyle. The inner, sealed-off chambers are filled with gas and control the shell's buoyancy. It can change depth by many metres, but rarely ventures into water shallower than 200m (655ft). The animal has a mouth, an eye, and 60–90 tentacles. It preys on crustaceans and fish.

The shell is fairly large and coiled and has an involute spire and a wide, gaping aperture. It is creamy white, with red-brown, flame-like radial bands and a black, callused area facing the aperture. The interior is nacreous. There is no umbilicus.

Widespread in the Southern Philippines, the shell is caught in nets suspended overnight. It is often polished and cut in half to reveal the chambers.

Argonautidae This is a family of octopus-like animals which do not produce a true shell. Females produce a false shell as an egg case. These species are found worldwide in warm seas.

1 *ARGONAUTA ARGO* **Common Paper Nautilus** *L. 1758* (to 20cm/8in) *Worldwide in warm seas. Seasonally* **C**. A thin, fragile, laterally compressed shell. It has a flat keel bearing two rows of many sharp nodules and there are radial wavy ridges. The shell is cream, but the early part of the keel is black or dark brown. Large, perfect specimens are rare.

2 *ARGONAUTA NODOSA* **Nodose Paper Nautilus** *Lightfoot 1786* (to 20cm/8in) *Indo-Pacific. Seasonally* **C**. This species is similar in shape to *Argonauta*

argo, but is rounded and more inflated and has a wider double keel and a slightly thicker shell. It is creamy white, with radiating rows of low, rounded tubercules. The early part of the keel is dark brown, the colour being darkest on the keel's nodules.

Spirulidae This one-species family consists of an internal shell carried in the posterior end of a small, squid-like creature which is distributed worldwide in warm seas.

3 *SPIRULA SPIRULA* **Common Spirula** *L. 1758* (3cm/1¼in) *Worldwide* **C**. A small, thin shell with loose spiral coils which are partitioned. It is pale-cream-ivory in colour and is often found washed up on beaches.

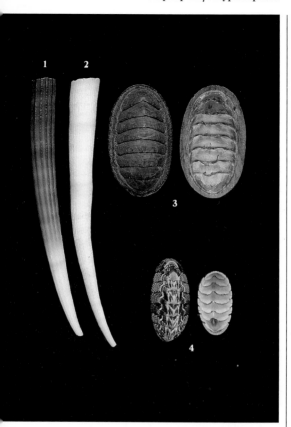

Class: Scaphopoda

Dentaliidae This is a small group consisting of shells with little or no variation. They are all slightly curved, tapering tubes, tusk-shaped and open at both ends. Distributed worldwide in sand in both shallow and deep water.

1 *DENTALIUM ELEPHANTINUM* **Elephant's Tusk Shell** *L. 1758* (8cm/3¼in) *Japan to Philippines* **C**. A solid, slightly curved shell with long, fairly coarse longitudinal ridges. It is dark green at the anterior end, white posteriorly.

2 *FISSIDENTALIUM VERNEDEI* **Vernede's Tusk** *Sowerby 1860* (10cm/4in) *Japan to Philippines* **C**. A thick, heavy, tapering shell, slightly curved and with fine, longitudinal cords and an anal notch. It is cream yellow.

Class: Polyplacophora

Chitonidae Chitons, or Coat-of-Mail Shells, are a group of molluscs with shells consisting of eight plates encircled by a muscular band or girdle, an arrangement which is reminiscent of the woodlouse. They inhabit rocky terrain and are vegetarian.

3 *AMAUROCHITON GLAUCUS Gray 1828* (5cm/2in) *S Australia* **C**. This shell is found at low tide under rocks. It has a minutely pustulose girdle and the plates are dark grey, with pale-blue undersides.

4 *CHITON TULIPA* **Tulip Chiton** *Quoy and Gaimard 1834* (3cm/1¼in) *South Africa* **C**. A medium-sized shell with a scaly girdle. The plates are strongly patterned with green, pink, and brown.

G L O S S A R Y

Terms in *italics* within a definition are defined separately.

Axis An imaginary line through the apex of gastropod shells around which the *whorls* revolve.

Body whorl The area of a shell which encloses its soft parts.

Byssus A cluster of thread-like filaments secreted by the inhabitants of some bivalve species and used to anchor the shell to other objects.

Calcareous White or chalky, due to calcium carbonate.

Cancellation A sculptured line on the surface of a shell which crosses others at right-angles, lattice-fashion. Also referred to as a reticulation.

Carina A pronounced ridge or keel.

Columella The pillar surrounding the central *axis* in gastropod shells.

Cord A rope-like decoration on the surface of a shell.

Corneous Horny.

Coronated Having *nodules* on the shoulders.

Crenulation A notch or scallop-like indentation on the ridge or *margins* of a shell.

Denticulate A small, tooth-like projection often occurring around the *margins* or inside the lip of a shell. A shell with such projections is described as denticulate or dentate.

Dorsum The back of a shell.

Fasciole A spiral band reflecting successive growth stages, found on the *siphonal canal* in some gastropods.

Frondose Leaf-like.

Fusiform Spindle-shaped.

Globose Rounded, almost spherical.

Inflated Swollen. Often used of the body whorl.

Keel A prominent, often flat, ridge.

Lamella A thin scale or plate on the surface of a shell.

Lira A fine ridge in the sculpturing of a shell.

Lunule A depressed area in front of the *umbones* of bivalves.

Margin The periphery of a shell.

Nacreous Having the qualities of mother-of-pearl.

Nodule A rounded or sharp node or knob.

Operculum A structure, usually round or oval, found on the foot of many gastropods with which the aperture is sealed after the inhabitant withdraws inside.

Ovate Oval-shaped.

Pallial line The curved scar line in a bivalve produced by the attachment of the inhabitant's mantle to the shell.

Pallial sinus The indentation in the *pallial line* of a bivalve indicating the former position of the retracted siphons.

Parietal shield In gastropod shells the area above the *columella* just inside and outside the aperture and opposite the outer lip.

Pelagic Free-swimming and/or living in open water.

Periostracum The outer covering of many shells.

Plica A plait or fold on the *columella* of some gastropods.

Process Spines or projections.

Protoconch The embryonic shell forming the apex or tip of a gastropod.

Punctated Dotted with small sculptural depressions.

Pustule A small, rounded projection, usually smaller than a *tubercule*.

Pyriform Pear-shaped.

Radial Term used to describe the ray-like decoration or sculpturing diverging from the *umbones* of bivalves.

Reticulation An alternative term for cancellation.

Rib A broad, elevated or raised structure on a shell.

Shoulder The angulation of a *whorl* in a gastropod.

Siphonal canal A groove or channel, also referred to as a notch, at the anterior end of a gastropod through which the inhabitant extends its siphon.

Stria A fine line or groove on the surface of a shell which in some cases reflects growth stages.

Stromboid notch In shells of the Strombus family, a deep notch above the *siphonal canal* through which the eye stalk of the inhabitant protrudes.

Suture A line or groove formed at the junction of the *whorls* of a gastropod.

Tent markings Pattern of exterior markings found mostly in cone shells. Also referred to as tenting.

Toxodont In bivalves, having teeth in rows which are transverse or oblique to the hinge plate.

Trigonal Triangulate: having three sides.

Tubercule A rounded projection on the surface of a shell usually larger than a *pustule* but smaller than a *nodule*.

Umbilicus The open *axis* around which the inner surface of a gastropod is coiled.

Umbo The earliest-formed part of a bivalve. Referred to in the plural as umbones. Also known as a beak.

Varix A thick ridge formed at the ridge of a shell's outer lip while it is resting from growth.

Veliger A mollusc at its free-swimming, larval stage.

Whorl A complete coil of a gastropod.

I N D E X

INDEX

INDEX

INDEX

INDEX

11. Dec. 06 Gift COOys